PROBLEMS OF AMERICAN SOCIETY
Bernard Rosenberg, General Editor

Criminal Justice

Criminal Justice

ABRAHAM S. BLUMBERG

Quadrangle Books | *Chicago*

To Mildred

Preface

Social scientists have generally shown little interest in the patterns that structure our system of criminal justice. Research is occasionally prompted by public furor over crime waves or scandals in the administration of criminal justice. But almost as quickly as the public outcry for reform subsides, concern for further scientific inquiry diminishes to near zero. Most social scientists (and even most lawyers) harbor latent feelings of contempt for the system of criminal justice and those engaged in it. They recall their own often unpleasant encounters with legal institutions (perhaps the traffic court or divorce tribunal) and either view the criminal court with ambivalence or simply dismiss it as a hopeless blot on the social landscape. Even in our law schools, criminal law receives short shrift: a one-semester course in a three-year curriculum. In part, this treatment reflects the fact that in the hierarchy of legal practitioners the criminal lawyer is hardly respectable.

We might expect political scientists, who have always shown a strong concern with legal institutions, to be interested in the criminal court. But political scientists almost never focus their at-

tention upon any court other than the United States Supreme Court
and its justices. The published opinions, the relative visibility of
the judicial incumbents, and a grandiose historical matrix in which
it functions, make the Supreme Court an exciting subject for political scientists. Big decisions with a sweeping and dramatic social
impact are more attractive for study than the dreary and often
prosaic subject matter of the lower courts. Political scientists, like
lawyers themselves, have for the most part concerned themselves
with historical, legal, and constitutional issues. Thus the fruit of
their work deals largely with court procedures, the niceties of intricate legal doctrine, studies of judicial personnel painted in the
grand tradition, and morphological descriptions which seldom go
beyond formal and explicit legal etiquette. These efforts add very
little to our knowledge of how the legal system works, nor have
they stimulated the gathering of facts which would sharpen and
enrich our insights into its social structure.

Indeed, as this book goes to press, the long-awaited reports of
the President's Commission on Law Enforcement and Administration of Justice, "The Challenge of Crime in a Free Society," and
the accompanying "Task Force Report: The Courts," have appeared. These research documents represent an extraordinary investment of money, resources, time, and the labors of the nation's
outstanding experts who have carefully set forth their recommendations based upon elaborate data. Regrettably, they add little
to what has already appeared in print in the way of criticism and
suggestions for the reform of the administration of criminal justice
in America.

Some of the remedies proposed in the reports would further
diminish the possibility of an adversary system of justice in favor
of one that is administratively convenient. Still other recommendations, if implemented, would reinforce the already quite
powerful bureaucratic apparatus of the criminal court while claim-
ing to be of greater service to the defendant. In the main, the
President's Commission reports deal with the formal, the legal, the
structural—and virtually ignore the reality of the criminal court

as a social system, as a community of human beings who are engaged in doing certain things with, to, and for each other.

We know the legal aspects of the process, but how shall we describe the social organization of the institutional mechanism which fastens the label "criminal" on the individual? We may be surprised to learn that formal legal structures, procedures, and rules are not ultimately significant in discerning the nature of the criminal court. Instead, the complex of organizational variables which defines the criminal court's social system and its inter-related occupational and bureaucratic networks is the key to its apprehension.

Sociology has traditionally been concerned with every aspect of that general area of human activity known as "crime." Sociologists in the classical tradition have carefully examined deviance and norm violation as a source of data for the study of society, but they have never had more than a peripheral interest in the criminal court. In part, sociological naiveté has produced this paradox. By virtually ignoring the criminal court, sociologists dismiss as inconsequential the crucial institutional variable in the area of crime. How can sociologists continue to study crime without inspecting the structure and process of the crime labeling mechanism itself?

Nor have criminologists made any important contributions to the field in recent years. Criminology texts in this century read almost as though they were written by the same person, or by members of the same committee—ritualized in content and style. The opening chapters invariably deal with several warmed-over, stock issues: the difficulty of defining what is a crime and who is a criminal, the possibilities of criminology becoming a science, the wretched state of criminal statistics and the inadequate means used to gather them. Then follow shopworn chapters on biological, psychological, social-psychological, social—and so on—sources of crime causation. Inevitably the author sets forth his own causation schema, after all the other demons have been properly analyzed, demolished, and interred.

Shortly before the closing chapters, which usually deal with prisons and the various philosophies of treatment and punishment, and inserted almost as an anti-climax, there is a lackadaisical treatment of the police and the courts. The policeman's lot is an unhappy one, we are told, because of lack of professional training, the corruption of political influence, overzealousness in seeking convictions, and a poor relationship with the public whose cooperation he must have. If the role of the police in the labeling process is given short shrift, the analysis of the criminal court is almost ludicrous. In large measure it recapitulates Hollywood-type clichés about courts and their personnel. Prominent in the scenario are ruthless district attorneys, shyster lawyers, stupid or incompetent judges, and inadequate psychiatrists and probation officers. All in all, the criminal court would appear to be a rather sleazy affair, wherein possibly corrupt officials permit guilty offenders to "cop out" to lesser offenses. This caricature is quite generally interlarded with succinct bits of jailhouse legalism and definitions of such terms as indictment, grand jury, misdemeanor, felony, arraignment, and so forth.

Coupled with the failings of sociologists to get at the really hard issues is the reluctance of the legal profession to entertain investigation and analysis. Unlike the prison, hospital, factory, school, or small town, the criminal court is truly a closed community. This is more than just the usual case of bureaucratic "secrets" which are fanatically defended from outside view. Even the press is zealously determined to report only that which will not offend a court's board of judges or the office of the prosecutor, in return for privileges granted in the past and to be granted in the future. The simple explanation is one of an ongoing system, dealing with delicate, tension- and trauma-producing law enforcement and administration, which requires the almost pathological distrust of "outsiders." Only court "regulars" are really accepted; others are treated routinely and in almost a coldly correct manner.

As a consequence, any effort to "study" the social structure of a court using routine methods would be futile. Members of the various occupational roles, if only in terms of their own work experience, are deeply suspicious of—almost hostile to—any effort to unearth embarrassing material. In their daily activity they have learned a first principle from the clients the court serves, namely, that too often the fact that he "talked too much" meant conviction for an accused person.

This virtually hostile attitude toward "outsiders" is in large measure a psychological defense against the inherent deficiencies of assembly-line justice, so characteristic of our major criminal courts. Intolerably large case loads, which must be handled with limited resources and personnel, potentially subject the participants in the court community to harsh scrutiny from appellate courts and other public and private sources of condemnation. Thus there is an almost irreconcilable conflict: intense pressures to process large numbers of cases, on the one hand, and the stringent ideological and legal requirements of "due process of law," on the other. The dilemma is frequently resolved through bureaucratically ordained short cuts, deviations, and outright rule violations by members of the court, from judges to stenographers, in order to meet production norms. Because they fear criticism on ethical as well as legal grounds, all the significant participants in the court's social structure are bound into an organized system of complicity. Patterned, covert, informal breaches, and evasions of "due process" are accepted as routine—they are institutionalized—but are nevertheless denied to exist.

These institutionalized evasions will be found to some degree in all criminal courts. Their nature, scope, and complexity are determined largely by the size of the court and the character of the community in which it is located—for example, whether it is a large, urban institution or a relatively small rural county court. When the social scientist appears on the scene to observe, to interview, and to collect "field data," he is often presented with a series of Potemkin villages for analysis.

This is a case study of a major American criminal court system. For convenience I call it Metropolitan Court. It is not a single court but a series of interrelated criminal courts dealing with criminal charges ranging from minor infractions of the law to felonies. Metropolitan Court is one of the largest criminal courts in the country in terms of case volume and personnel employed. The data have a national applicability because many of the organizational and occupational characteristics found in the Metropolitan Court setting can be seen in criminal courts throughout the country.

Much of the data was gathered during the course of nearly twenty years of work in almost every activity related to the administration of the criminal law, including the practice of law. Almost five years before the close of that period, when I decided that I wanted to record my observations about the American system of criminal justice, I began systematically to interview most of the personnel and officials conducting business in Metropolitan Court. During five years I interviewed and re-interviewed approximately two hundred persons to check out my observations and conclusions. I talked with most of the lawyers, probation officers, court clerks, psychological and psychiatric personnel, and district attorneys of the court, and other officials, such as parole officers, who may only occasionally conduct business in Metropolitan Court. I read more than two thousand psychiatric and probation reports, interviewed in detail more than seven hundred felony defendants about their court experience, and observed approximately three hundred trials and over fifteen hundred pleas of guilty to a lesser offense, including some of the preliminary negotiations involved. In addition, during the summers of 1960 through 1965, I visited criminal courts in some of the major urban areas of the country, as well as several rural courts in the New England area.

My purpose is to examine some of the traditional assumptions and venerated ideas of the American legal system as embodied in the criminal court. These consist of bits of legal conventional wisdom which, when strung together, precariously comprise the system's myth structure. Repeated often enough, they appear to be the real thing, and whoever questions them becomes at worst a knave, at best an iconoclast, a cynic, or perhaps a polemicist.

The fundamental myth of the institutionalized system of criminal justice is the assertion that "ours is the accusatorial as opposed to the inquisitorial system." We point with pride to our rejection of methods of coercion, be they savage or subtle, in securing convictions. Instead, the burden is upon the state to procure independent evidence to establish an individual's guilt. Another myth is that the system of bargain justice, of pleading to a lesser plea—"plea copping," or what I prefer to call "justice by negotiation" —meets the standards of due process of law because the defendant freely and willingly pleads guilty in open court. A further myth is that the policing, prosecuting, judging, evaluating, and defending functions are haphazardly decentralized and do not have any firm interconnection. Still another myth is that judges are not part of the bargain plea process, that they are not involved in procuring pleas. The most damaging myth (most damaging, that is, to believing defendants) is that criminal lawyers are engaged in *defending* clients; that ours is an adversary system of criminal justice —although claims of the combative features of the state versus the accused are seldom subjected to close scrutiny. Finally, there is the myth that probation and psychiatry, as "helping" professions in the court setting, serve both the defendant and the court organization in furnishing objective, impartial evaluations and reports.

Occupational and organizational ideologies, like political ideologies, die hard. A court's job incumbents and members of the legal profession develop a vested interest and an intellectual commitment which inevitably tend to distort their perspectives. So much so that one outstanding scholar refers to the criminal court as "this veritable mansion." But here we shall be examining and analyzing a system of justice by negotiation. Because of the formidable array of organizational structure, personnel, and power of the criminal court, the accusation of the defendant can be tantamount to conviction.

In this book I shall deal with the office of the prosecutor and the police only peripherally. They represent distinct organizations characterized by ideologies, values, goals, and styles unique to their function. Together they are part of an elaborate process which may result in an individual becoming an accused person who is then presented to the criminal court. Where prosecution and police functions touch the internal court structure and the court's decisions, this will be noted. But my primary focus and concern is with the court's apparatus itself, and my central question is: What can one expect *after* the decision to prosecute has been made by police and prosecution?

No book is ever the product of a single mind, and I wish to acknowledge a number of intellectual debts. I am grateful to Bernard Rosenberg, who sparked the whole project some years ago; to Israel Gerver, who introduced me to the sociological angle of vision; to Alexander B. Smith, who has been a constant source of encouragement as well as a helpful irritant; and to Arthur Vidich and Joseph Bensman, who contributed magnanimously of their time and offered valuable criticisms and insights, and who helped clarify some of the basic ideas in the work. Finally, I am greatly indebted to the defendants of Metropolitan Court, who did much to fill the more obvious gaps in my legal education.

Contents

Preface *vii*

1 The Criminal Court as a Social Problem *3*

2 The Twilight of the Adversary System *13*

3 The Criminal Court as Organization and
   Communication System *39*

4 Discipline and Perspective in the Criminal Court *73*

5 The Lawyer as Agent-Mediator *95*

6 The Judge as Bureaucrat *117*

7 Probation and Psychiatry *143*

8 The Convergence of the Adversary and
   Bureaucratic Models *169*

Notes *185*

Index 199

| Criminal Justice |

1

The criminal court as a social problem

> "I understand it."
>
> "No, you don't. Every man's supposed to have certain rights."
>
> "Certain inalienable rights," Starke said, "to liberty, equality and the pursuit of happiness. I learnt it in school, as a kid."
>
> "Not that," Prew said. "That's the Constitution. Nobody believes that any more."
>
> "Sure they do," Starke said. "They all believe it. They just don't do it. But they believe it."
>
> "Sure," Prew said. "That's what I mean."
>
> "But at least in this country they believe it," Starke said, "even if they don't do it. . . ."
>
> —James Jones, *From Here to Eternity*

In his landmark work, *An American Dilemma,* Gunnar Myrdal describes an important source of strain in American life: what he calls the American Creed—embodying notions of equality, justice, democracy, rule of law, and Christian brotherhood which "ought to rule"—is flagrantly evaded in the case of the Negro. As a social institution, the criminal court contains elements of a similar dilemma. While the constitutional ideology of due process and rule of law is proclaimed as the mode of justice we exalt and revere, it is a perfunctory, administrative-bureaucratic version of due process that has been implemented in our criminal courts. "Bureaucratic due process" serves as bland obeisance to constitutional principles. It is characterized by the superficial ceremonies and formal niceties of traditional due process, but not its substance. It consists of strategies and evasions calculated to induce pleas of guilty, and it has become the truly viable system of criminal justice in America.

The precise, legalistic formulations of due process of law are thought to be the bedrock of the basic institutional mission of the adult criminal court. That mission, stated quite simply, is to answer authoritatively and in a "civilized" fashion a single question: Is the accused innocent or guilty? Historically, the answer was arrived at through a formal adversary procedure bound by strict rules of evidence and the all-embracing constitutional limitations of due process, culminating in a trial by jury. The traditional forms of due process were articulated by values and concerns reflecting the pursuit of individualism and individual rights. Bureaucratic due process has other objectives which tend to exalt the goals and requirements of the court organization itself.

Of course, the characteristic features of the old world which generated the rules of traditional due process no longer exist. Due process and its requirements may indeed be incompatible with the inevitable secular and impersonal criteria of excellence and efficiency inherent in modern large-scale organization. Some important evidence on this point is the decline of the jury system and the elaborate array of structure and personnel in the criminal courts, which exert pressures to accomplish an overwhelming number of guilty pleas.

The meticulous requisites and goals of due process include, among other things, a presumption of innocence and a truly adversary proceeding, in the course of which an accused person receives a full, fair, and open judicial hearing or trial. The hearing must be a real one, not a sham or some contrived pretense. The proceedings from arrest to sentence must be free from any taint of coercion or threats, no matter how subtle they may appear. But in fact, the rational-instrumental goals of the court organization, in its urgent demand for guilty pleas, have produced a bargain-counter, assembly-line system of criminal justice which is incompatible with traditional due process. The dilemma is sharpened by the fact that the concern for the individual envisioned and postulated by the rules of due process in determining guilt or innocence, is no longer present at this crucial level. Instead, the concern, if any, appears at the post-guilt, pre-sentence stage, while the actual determination of guilt is arrived at through perfunctory ministerial procedures which have become the hallmark of the criminal court's rationality.

The dilemma and its implications may be seen in still another way: the concepts of "due process" and "rule of law" are frequently used interchangeably and have assumed the quality of ritual affirmations. They now have a distinct ideological character in that they distort or conceal some aspect of social reality. Their abstruse, mystical, and protean qualities have helped to obscure the emergence and institutionalization of bureaucratic due process, culminating in a state of affairs in which the overwhelming majority of defendants now plead guilty before trial. What passes for a full, fair, and open "hearing" are the secret negotiation sessions which become forever submerged in the final plea of guilty and are therefore rarely subject to routine examination or review.

The rule of law is not self-executing. It is translated into reality by men in institutions. Traditional constitutional elements of criminal law, when placed in the institutional setting of a modern criminal court, are reshaped by a bureaucratic organization to serve its requirements and goals. In pursuit of production and efficiency, the criminal court's formal and informal organizations have harnessed the court's ideology, structure, and personnel to overcome and alter the rules and safeguards of constitutional due process. The meandering judicial effort to articulate more protective rules of due process (to protect against police coercion, unlawful search, wiretapping, lack of counsel, and so on) has simply shunted attention away from the inadequacies and harshness of the criminal court as an institutional arrangement. The vague and constantly shifting constitutional requirements of due process have allowed the rational, impersonal, and ruthless criteria of modern organizational life to gain primacy, so that the individual accused is minimized and given short shrift. The void created by the historical obscurities and indefiniteness of due process has been filled with definitions that are favorable and peculiar to the bureaucratic world-view, its felt necessities, values, and priorities. The "adversary system" and the "presumption of innocence" are compromised in the framework of the formal court process itself. They are supplanted by a non-adversary, accusatory system which actually favors a presumption of guilt.

Three relatively recent items reported in the *New York Times* underscore this aspect of the matter as it has manifested itself in one of the major criminal courts. In one instance the Bronx County Bar Association condemned "mass assembly-line justice," which was rushing defendants into pleas of guilty and into convictions "in violation of their legal rights." [1] Another item reports the unusual event of a judge criticizing his own court system (the New York Criminal Court) to the effect that "pressure to set statistical records in disposing of cases had hurt the administration of justice." [2] A third, a most unusual recent public discussion in the press in this regard, was a statement by a leading New York appellate judge decrying "instant justice" which is employed to reduce court calendar congestion, "converting our courthouses into counting houses . . . as in most big cities where the volume of business tends to overpower court facilities." [3]

A noted legal scholar, Herbert L. Packer, has recently analyzed our system of criminal justice in terms of a two-model process.[4] The first he calls a "crime control model." This version of criminal justice presumes the guilt of the accused and operates with assembly-line speed and efficiency to process large numbers of defendants. The crime control model balances the interests of the individual and society, and individual interests must often give way. The other system is the "due process model." Here the system of criminal justice is a legalistic obstacle course to serve the needs and rights of individual defendants. The emphasis is on concern for the individual and on quality at the expense of quantity. Packer indicates that a really efficient system of criminal justice based on the crime control model would be repressive, and he concludes that the trend in America is toward the due process model.

A leading constitutional authority, Yale Kamisar, describing the system of criminal justice, distinguishes between what he describes as "The Show in the Gatehouse vs. The Show in the Mansion." In using the term "gatehouse," he refers to the coercive, inquisitorial practices used by the police, prosecutors, and others to harass defendants into confessions.

> In this "gatehouse" of American criminal procedure—through which most defendants journey and beyond which many never get—the enemy of the state is a depersonalized "subject" to be "sized up" . . . he is "game" to be stalked and cornered. Here ideals are checked at the door. . . . Once he leaves the "gatehouse" and enters the "mansion" . . . the enemy of the state is repersonalized, even dignified, the public invited, and a stirring ceremony in honor of individual freedom from law enforcement celebrated.[5]

Kamisar is almost lyrical in proclaiming the "safety . . . the comfort of this veritable mansion" (the criminal court) as he intones its virtues in contrast to the ruthless, sordid activities of the keepers of the "gatehouse."

Neither of these inquiries into the nature of the criminal process reflects reality. They offer ideal types in that they do not *fully* describe some portion of reality. As ideal types they may be used as vehicles to learn about reality, but they are not reality itself. Despite recent judicial amplification of individual rights under due process, the system of criminal justice does not operate on the basis of a crime control or due process model, nor is the criminal court a veritable mansion.

SOME LIMITATIONS OF EXISTING DATA

In fifty-two separate jurisdictions, including the District of Columbia and the federal government, there is a bewildering variety of criminal courts. Those of so-called "inferior jurisdiction" are variously known as police courts, magistrates' courts, peace courts, recorders' courts, mayors' courts, city courts, special sessions courts, quarter sessions courts, and municipal courts. These deal with minor criminal violations of state and local laws and ordinances (usually misdemeanors) such as drunkenness, traffic violations, simple assaults, petty thefts, disorderly conduct, prostitution, homosexuality, possession of drugs, and a wide range of other offenses ranging from begging alms to evading payment of fare on public transportation. Those courts dealing with more serious offenses, usually felonies (for example, murder, arson, kidnaping, robbery, burglary, and the more serious assaults), are variously called county courts, superior courts, supreme courts, district courts, or circuit courts.

The major distinction between a felony and a misdemeanor is in the nature of the punishment imposed. In the case of a felony the punishment may be death or imprisonment for usually more than one year in a state prison. A misdemeanor includes any other offense for which punishment is less severe, and imprisonment in a local jail or workhouse. The states differ widely in defining, prosecuting, and punishing felonies and misdemeanors, so the terms are not very useful in describing specific criminal conduct.[6]

At best there is a confusion of courts overlapping in their jurisdictions and a complete lack of uniformity about names, functions,
usages, and reporting practice. The character of local political arrangements, customs, social perspectives, and community resources
often in large measure determines not only what activity will be
labeled "criminal," but the data-reporting practices and the socio-
legal process as well. There are generally four distinct levels of
courts in the various jurisdictions. The first level holds preliminary
hearings on serious cases—felonies which it sends on to the second
level—but it renders final disposition for minor and petty offenses.
The second level conducts trials on serious charges and disposes
of these cases; it is usually the highest court of original jurisdiction
in a state. The third level generally represents the intermediate
court to which appeals are carried. The fourth level is usually the
highest court in the state; it is usually called "Supreme Court" or
"Court of Appeals" and receives appeals from all the lower courts.
Cases may be appealed from here, if there are proper grounds, to
the United States Supreme Court.[7]

Each year millions of persons appear as defendants in our
criminal courts. Yet it is one of those strange ironies which persist
despite our wealth, power, and resources, that we know more
about the quality and quantity of detergents and dishwashers than
we do about the number of people in trouble with the law. We
have even less systematic information about their disposition and
treatment. The FBI, the central agency in the U.S. for the collection of crime statistics, reports that in 1964 there were 4,685,080
persons arrested in the United States for all offenses, not including traffic violations. But the figure is at best an understatement,
for it is drawn from 3,977 agencies reporting on an estimated
population of only 132,439,000.[8] Further, in every jurisdiction
many offenders are not necessarily processed in the criminal courts
but are handled administratively—for example, defendants released because of lack of evidence to prosecute, or lack of cooperation of the victim of a crime; defendants turned over to juvenile

authorities, or released with a warning, and so on. In all, the number of persons arrested in any year who finally reach the criminal court is a number considerably lower than total arrests.

The FBI concentrates its data-gathering efforts on offenses and arrests which are reported by local agencies to the FBI via fingerprint clearances. A summary of this data is published in July of each year, covering the previous year, in the format of the *Uniform Crime Reports*. The whole enterprise is heavily dependent upon the adequacy and veracity of police officials at the local level. They in turn are subject to cross-pressures which often cause them to manipulate crime statistics for their own local administrative purposes. A recent study of the American bail system estimates "that ten to twelve million Americans need bail bonds each year (for other than traffic cases)." [9] Regardless of the relative merits of any of these widely disparate and admittedly crude indices, the plain fact is that we do not really know precisely how many people are prosecuted in our criminal courts each year.

The only degree of administrative uniformity present in an otherwise chaotic situation is in the federal district courts, which in addition to their civil function deal with persons charged with federal offenses. Federal statistics, while they represent only a small proportion of those who appear in a criminal court in America during any given year, are at least accurate, unquestionably valid, and uniformly collected. [10]

Although Metropolitan Court is a system of interconnected courts which will serve as a model of this study, I shall be dealing largely with the "second level" or felony level of that court. It is important, therefore, within the scope of the limited data available, to fix the number of accused persons involved each year at the felony level, as they will constitute the population of our discussion. (But it must be emphasized that the subsequent analysis, except for minor details, is entirely applicable to the vast number of other persons who appear as defendants in connection with so-called lesser offenses or misdemeanors.) Probably the best estimate available is that of the American Bar Foundation, the research unit of the American Bar Association. It indicates that each year 300,000 persons appear in the second level type court, charged with crimes punishable by imprisonment of a year or more (usually felonies).[11] Of course this figure is dwarfed by the almost five million additional persons who appear each year in a criminal court charged with lesser offenses (misdemeanors other than traffic offenses).[12] None of the foregoing includes the approximately 600,000 children who appear each year as delinquency cases in our juvenile courts.[13]

Inadequate statistics are matched by the fact that we really know very little, apart from conventional legal statements and descriptions, of what happens to the single individual caught up in what may be the most devastating experience of his life. Even the individual who has experienced the criminal court as an accused has only a vague conception of the administrative apparatus which may deprive him of his freedom, or perhaps even irreparably damage him, his family, and his future work career.[14] If it is true that the quality of a nation's civilization can be largely measured by the methods it uses in the enforcement of its criminal law, then the criminal court as an institutional arrangement illustrates the fundamental erosion of the quality of life in our society. Beyond the well-defined ecological disorders of urban blight, pollution, congestion, and the other myriad ills of "ungovernable" communities, beyond the traditional social problems of poverty, psychosis, delinquency and the like, lie basic institutional changes. They proceed unobtrusively, but they reflect in more subtle fashion the character of the deterioration. Indeed, the system of criminal justice, and its institutional vehicle, the criminal court, reflects the specter that haunts America in the second half of the twentieth century—the impoverishment of institutional commitments to people. Government frequently does not serve the people, nor universities the students, nor production the consumer; similarly, there has been a debasement of the criminal court's traditional commitments to the clients it serves. Whether one is a defendant in a criminal court, an applicant for unemployment insurance, or an outpatient at a clinic, when one receives short shrift or is routinized, or treated perfunctorily—or even with arrogant harshness—he considers these private misfortunes a consequence of his lowly status. Very few individuals ever perceive their private troubles as in any way related to the possible weaknesses of social institutions. We have been told far too often that "the fault, dear Brutus, lies not in our stars but in ourselves."

2

The twilight of the adversary system

> "My guiding principle is this: guilt is never
> to be doubted."
> —Franz Kafka, *In the Penal Colony*

Many of the troubles of the criminal court stem in part from the
Supreme Court's original position, before the Civil War, that no
part of the Bill of Rights should act as a restriction upon the
states.[1] Certain guarantees of the law were thus available to individuals only in federal cases. This has been further complicated
by the fact that historically a majority of Supreme Court justices
has resisted the incorporation of the specific guarantees of the
Bill of Rights through the Fourteenth Amendment, so as not to
permit them to apply to the states. There has been a good deal
of controversy as to the precise meaning and application of the
Fourteenth Amendment.[2] Regardless of the merit of the various
arguments, the fact is that the Supreme Court has haltingly and
almost reluctantly used the Fourteenth Amendment to apply many
of the features of the Bill of Rights against the states. Although

many states had earlier adopted many of the federal constitutional requirements of criminal procedure, their implementation and administration has been at best haphazard, uneven, and often undermined by local action. In a long, attritionary process spanning almost a century, the Supreme Court has been responsible for many of the procedural reforms of our local systems of criminal justice. In the absence of congressional legislation to implement the due process clause of the Fourteenth Amendment, the court has assumed the vital role of legislating in this area.[3] Indeed, it has been necessary for the court, from time to time, to reverse its own rulings in order to bring the states in line with more rigorous federal standards.

As a consequence of these constitutional strictures, the Supreme Court proceeded to weave an intricate web of legal niceties, until as a practical matter two discrete systems of criminal justice emerged.[4] Distinct state and federal standards persisted until relatively recently, both derived from the Bill of Rights dilemma. The first eight amendments to the Constitution were designed to protect the individual from a potentially oppressive central government. The Fourth, Fifth, Sixth, and Eighth Amendments, however, are of main importance in regulating federal criminal proceedings. These amendments concern illegal searches and seizures, self-incrimination, indictment by grand jury, trial by jury, double jeopardy, excessive bail, and cruel and unusual punishments. The right to confrontation by accusers and witnesses is guaranteed, as is the right to the assistance of counsel. In short, some of the basic general requirements of "due process of law" are spelled out.

Included in the Fifth Amendment of the Bill of Rights and in the Fourteenth Amendment are the omnibus due process clauses. Quite generally, these have been defined to mean that when the government (state or federal) proceeds against a person for some alleged violation of the law, the accused person must be accorded the full measure of "fairness" and all the procedural safeguards of those "minimal standards which are of the very essence of a scheme of ordered liberty." [5] Due process means further, "those canons of decency and fairness which express the notions of justice." [6] While meanings of "due process" and "justice" remain vague, ill-defined, and elusive, reflections on the issue of what is meant by the terms appear to polarize about notions of "fair" and "unfair." [7] The notion of due process is the criterion in determining whether a "democratic" state has acted properly or arbitrarily in a legal proceeding. Due process then, while it bears the same sense of obscurity, the same chimerical quality and equivocation of meaning as does "justice," refers simply to the application of "just" legal norms in the resolution of controversies between individuals and between the individual and the state, in a "fair" and "reasonable" manner.[8]

Historically, the federally accused defendant in effect will be accorded all of the precise prescriptive safeguards of "fairness" as spelled out in the Bill of Rights—and then some. But a state defendant may be accorded *less* than the exacting requirements of the Bill of Rights. As long as the procedures employed by a state do not violate some aspect of due process which the Supreme Court, at the time of a review, considers to be "fundamental rights," they will be found adequate. Generally, then, the court has been loath to upset local patterns of the criminal process, if these meet the court's current notions of "minimal standards which are of the very essence of a scheme of ordered liberty."

THE MEANDERING JOURNEY OF DUE PROCESS

The Supreme Court has argued heatedly within itself over the meaning of due process in a state criminal case. Justice Frankfurter often stated what has been the majority position, namely, that due process can mean more than the Bill of Rights and often much less. Justice Black has forcefully asserted that "due process" is a shorthand transcript for the Bill of Rights, and no less than that.[9] The intellectual underpinning of the limited application of federal due process rules lies in the intricate niceties of federalism and the accompanying constitutional allocation of powers among the states. The central theme in that context of constitutional thought is the notion that in a "federal system," local and regional norms of "justice" and "fair play" must be permitted full latitude for their development and implementation. Thus those institutional arrangements which are peculiar to a particular state or region are to be respected as an important feature of our federal system of government. Apart from the political and legal features of federalism which reflect a pervasive distrust of strong central governments, the concept also embodies a tacit recognition of the fact that America is not a homogeneous nation. On the contrary, the nation's distinct regional character is thereby constitutionally recognized.

For example, so long as a state's particular rules of criminal procedure do not violate "those fundamental principles of liberty and justice which lie at the base of all our civil and political institutions," [10] even though they may depart from federal procedures, they will be permitted to stand. The "standards" of due process in criminal procedure have been, in the main, fairly explicit with regard to the federal authority, but significantly less so with regard to the states. Failure to impose upon the states the obligation to incorporate all the explicit constitutional requirements of federal criminal procedure has resulted in a time consuming, cumbersome ritual in which the Supreme Court examines each situation, case by case, to determine whether a current standard of due process has been met.

The most dramatic illustration for our time that the definition, quality, and character of "due process," "rule of law," and "justice" depend upon the current state of the collective conscience is the experience of the Negro in America. It has been a long, tortuous, and painful development from "separate but equal" to a perspective that mere separation is unequal in social and legal terms. [11] The interpretation of due process and equal protection of the laws can be, and has been, tempered with whimsy and expedience. Despite noble historical assertions, this concept which is at the root of our criminal law administration remains a very personal, subjective, and idiosyncratic device to be used to satisfy the felt needs of the moment. It is often shaped by events, personal anxieties, social and economic biases, and predilections of judges and administrators.

Because due process has evolved largely by a circuitous process of inclusion, exclusion, and modification of rules and standards, some rather bizarre and paradoxical results have emerged. Thus, in one instance, where a suspected narcotics seller had been arrested, the police forcibly pumped the suspect's stomach and made him swallow an emetic to retrieve two morphine capsules which were later used as evidence to convict him. The Supreme Court was shocked and overturned the conviction.[12] The court thought the conduct of the police had exceeded the restraints imposed by constitutional prohibitions against "unreasonable" searches and compulsory self-incrimination. But five years later the court thought the taking of a blood sample of a suspect while he was unconscious, as evidence to be used against him, did not violate notions of due process.[13] Similarly, in 1966 the court decided that taking a blood sample against a person's will, to determine whether he was drunk while driving, did not violate the due process privilege against self-incrimination.[14] Conceivably, the decisions in the latter two cases are a product of the fact that in both instances serious motor vehicle accidents were involved wherein the drivers had been drinking.

DUE PROCESS AND RULE OF LAW AS COERCIVE INSTRUMENTS

What the exigencies of war and crisis can do to the "rule of law," "justice," and "due process" is best exemplified by a now almost forgotten incident in American jurisprudence: the exclusion of Japanese-Americans from the West Coast and their removal to "relocation centers" during World War II. Despite later claims of military necessity and danger of sabotage, it was not for several months after the attack upon Pearl Harbor that Executive Order 9066 was issued on February 19, 1942, authorizing the appropriate military commanders and civilian authorities to prescribe military areas where persons could be detained or from which they could be excluded.[15] On March 21, 1942, Congress established criminal penalties for violation of the executive order. The actual order excluding all the Japanese from their homes in California, Washington, Oregon, and parts of Arizona was not promulgated until May 3, 1942, and they were not actually removed to interior locations until October 1942. On the basis of "military necessity," some 112,000 persons of Japanese ancestry, more than seventy thousand of whom were American citizens, were subject to these harsh penalties without any prior legal or administrative determination as to their guilt or innocence in connection with sabotage or other acts of disloyalty. The sole criterion employed in the determination of one's being subject to these measures was quite simply racial descent.

The Supreme Court, which tended to gloss over some of the thorny constitutional issues involved, upheld the curfew and "relocation" restrictions on the basis of findings of "military urgency" by the executive branch.[16] The affirmation of the exclusion and relocation regulations, and their accompanying criminal sanctions in the Korematsu case, came approximately nine months before World War II ended. There could no longer have been any justification for the repressive measures because of the nature of the "emergency." A constitutional scholar suggests that the basis of these unprecedented measures lay in pressures exerted by West Coast hysteria.[17] Another authority observes that the justices were loath to invoke any of the constitutional niceties in thwarting military power; they avoided the serious constitutional issues; the court's conduct was "a matter for debate." [18] An appropriate footnote to the affair is the fact that from December 7, 1941, to the end of hostilities not a single person of Japanese descent (citizen or otherwise) was found guilty of any act of sabotage or espionage.[19]

The law is hydra-headed and can serve many masters in inconsistent ways. It waits only for a "moral entrepreneur" and an "enforcer" to call up violators and deviants, or undesirable and unpopular persons who have been heretofore overlooked or not so designated.[20] "Moral entrepreneurs" legislate new norms or moral codes which are then applied by society's "enforcers," both having agreed in their respective spheres of action that certain patterns of conduct or persons are odious.

To presume that "law" and "justice" are instruments possible only in certain kinds of societies (i.e., "democratic") is a fanciful oversimplification. Modern totalitarian societies, the ancient despotisms, modern democratic states—all have produced comprehensive juridical systems dispensing "justice." Rome was certainly a model of tyranny in antiquity, and it articulated a legal system which serves as the point of origin of many legal systems today. The Russia that emerged after the violent upheaval of 1917 thought it could then uproot and dispose of "capitalist law." But such early hopes were soon dashed on the granite realities of the felt necessities for some sort of legal code to regulate all aspects of conduct of the "soviet man" who was to emerge. Terror, naked force, and law merged to deal with "deviationists" and "counterrevolutionary crimes." In the Soviet legal system, law, especially the criminal law, serves as a form of consciousness. It is an instrument of the party in its effort to fashion the Soviet people into loyal, industrious citizens, respectful of the authority of the communist social order.[21]

Raul Hilberg carefully documents the use of the German juridical and bureaucratic apparatus by the Nazis to annihilate methodically a segment of humanity. Existing legal machinery, including the civil and criminal courts, was employed to effect three phases of the destruction process: definition, expropriation, and concentration of the Jews. The first phase dealt with the legal establishment of the answer to the question, "Who is a Jew?" and the judicial determination of all the legal consequences of such status for employment, marriage, and other individual rights and relationships. The second phase concerned itself with the legal and judicial procedures employed in stripping those who had been legally determined to be Jews of most of their property, including jobs, contracts, business enterprises, and personal wealth. The final step provided for the social isolation of the Jews through their total ghettoization by law, the legally compulsory termination of social relations between Jews and others, including elaborate laws relating to intermarriage, housing restrictions, regulations of their movement, and identification procedures. All these measures included severe criminal penalties for violators.[22]

Juridical systems, then, embody and personify particular interpretations of the collective conscience of a social order. The legal concept of due process serves much the same function in the legal system as does the joker in a card game: it has a shifting meaning and application. Just as the structure of legal and juridical systems are a reflection of group structure and the individuals who comprise it, so the content of due process of law (whether at the Supreme Court or state level) may have a particular meaning, purpose, and character that mirror the unique angle of vision of a historical and social location. In a rational-legal society, the "rule of law" is invoked as the source of legitimacy. In dealing with a wrongdoer, the question is not guilt or innocence but rather a demonstration of the "approved way" in which violence can be used legitimately vis-à-vis a given individual. In American society the "approved way" means due process of law, which in essence refers to the normatively established, institutionalized recipes for invoking and using legal machinery. As we have seen, the concept is not only not fixed, but its precise dimensions and boundaries are never fully clear and unambiguous. It is still evolving.

The Supreme Court's almost exclusive concern has been to generate a more perfect set of rules of due process to redress the

balance between the state and an accused. Even under optimal circumstances a criminal case is very much a one-sided affair, the
parties to the contest being decidedly unequal in strength and resources. But the concern with better and more extensive rules has
served as a façade of moral philosophy to divert our gaze from the
more significant development of the emergence of "bureaucratic
due process," a non-adversary system of justice by negotiation. It
consists of secret bargaining sessions, employing subtle, bureaucratically ordained modes of coercion and influence to dispose of
onerously large case loads in an efficacious and "rational" manner.
Except for isolated cases, the bargaining or "cop-out" procedures
on which our entire system of criminal law administration would
appear to depend have never been subjected to extensive judicial
scrutiny to determine their constitutionality or propriety in terms
of due process.[23]

THE CRIMINAL PROCESS: IDEOLOGIES, PRINCIPLES, AND PRACTICES

Society tries to develop social, legal, and organizational structures
which will filter out law violators and at the same time provide an
avenue of possible freedom to those who are innocent or simply
casual law-breakers.[24] The problems posed by the dilemma are
exacerbated by a society's stated ideological commitments, on the
one hand, and by the politics and competing interests of those involved in the system of administering the criminal law, on the other.

Hardly a term of the Supreme Court passes without some modification of the rules of due process, which in turn are made bind-
ing upon the states. The brief survey that follows is not intended
to be an exhaustive analysis of the constitutional issues and theories
involved. Instead, it examines some of the major themes of constitutionalism which serve as the ideological and legal underpinning for the criminal court's legitimacy. The legalistic rules of
"due process" are in large measure ideal expressions and do not
sensitize us to the reality of the criminal court process in its daily

operations. But they are of great interest because they underscore the hiatus between the stated rules and the operative realities. We can see what happens to them as they filter through the organizational structures designed for their enforcement.

Constitutional renovation in an effort to close the federal-state procedural gaps has been taking place so rapidly that legal comment is often obsolete by the time it appears in print. With this in mind, a cursory statement of certain principles of justice and fairness, including some specific "across the board" due process requirements, as they have been wrought in the courts and through statutes and the federal and state constitutions, may be stated as follows:

(1) *Definiteness of penal statutes and codes.* A criminal statute must establish a normative standard which is definite and unambiguously clear, to which one could adhere in structuring his future conduct.[25]

(2) *Accusation must give notice.* An accusation of crime can be a grand jury indictment, by an information, or by a complaint. It is important that the procedure employed actually inform the accused person of the precise nature of the charge being made so that he may prepare a defense.

(3) *Arraignment with all possible speed.* Although not always considered a due process requirement, an accused must be taken before a magistrate or similar official performing a judicial function so that charges made by police or other law enforcement officials may be reviewed to determine their propriety. It has often been thought that most violations of due process rules occur during what is considered to be the critical period between the arrest or apprehension of an individual and actual appearance in a court.

The so-called McNabb-Mallory rule requiring that arrested persons be taken "without unnecessary delay" to a hearing officer (a U.S. commissioner), where they will be advised of their rights to counsel and to remain silent, has not been followed by the states. Usually the state courts have dealt with the problem of "prompt production" of the arrested person by interpreting a violation of statutes in this area as simply another circumstance to consider in evaluating whether or not a subsequent confession was voluntary. Thus, delay for purposes of interrogation and confession has been tacitly encouraged in the past.[26] It is during this interval that confessions are said to be elicited through various forms of administrative guile and coercion, and during which overzealous detaining officials may act arbitrarily and, indeed, unlawfully.

Some of the best-known police manuals suggest some rather cynical ruses and ploys for the questioning of accused persons.[27] These include feigning sympathy and solicitude for an accused; falsely identifying him as a perpetrator of other crimes so that he will confess to the offense being investigated; playing two or more suspects off against one another and indicating that one has confessed; emphasizing to the accused that his "nervousness" indicates his guilt, by calling attention to the dryness of his mouth or other obviously common emotional symptoms of stress. In all, some rather reprehensible activities which fall far short of threats and outright coercion have in the past been possible and constitutional at the pre-arraignment stage. Since *Escobedo vs. Illinois* (1964), and *Miranda vs. Arizona* (1966), interrogation of suspected persons without their consent, unless a defense attorney is present, is forbidden. As a consequence, all confessions except those which are absolutely spontaneous and unsolicited, may be outlawed, unless there has been a knowing waiver of one's rights to remain silent.[28]

(4) *The privilege against self-incrimination.*[29] This principle would include not only all confessions, as indicated above, but also those induced by the more subtle instances of manipulation and psychological harassment, periods of long interrogation, and the forcible taking of breath tests or certain other bodily evidence. The historical basis for these requirements was a reaction to the Inquisition, the Court of Star Chamber, and other instances wherein self-incrimination of various kinds has been employed. For

example, in *Leyra vs. Denno* (1954), a confession was obtained by a psychiatrist with a knowledge of hypnosis. He had been introduced to Leyra (the defendant) as a physician who would treat him for his physical complaints. Leyra's subsequent confessions and admissions of guilt to the psychiatrist were thrown out as violative of due process.

The self-incrimination provisions of the Fifth Amendment ("no person . . . shall be compelled in any criminal case to be a witness against himself . . .") do *not* offer protection against being fingerprinted, photographed, having one's measurements taken, writing or speaking for identification, appearing in court, standing, walking, or making a particular gesture.

(5) *Prohibition against unreasonable searches and seizures.* This requirement underlines the right of an individual to be immune from arrests which are not based on the probability that he has actually committed a crime. In addition, searches and seizures of property, in the absence of a warrant or probable cause, to be used as evidence later, is also forbidden under the Fourth Amendment.[30]

(6) *The right to the assistance of counsel.* The emphasis on "assistance" is crucial in view of the perfunctoriness of counsel in the routinized procedures of "assembly-line justice" so characteristic of our criminal courts. Not until 1963, after more than thirty years of judicial debate, was it decided that this constitutional requirement applies across the board to the states in all felony trials involving indigent defendants.[31] Before there had been a patchquilt of provisions under which the various states would, according to their own laws, furnish counsel to an indigent person who could not afford private counsel.[32] It is now fairly clear that, regardless of one's financial capacity, the right to have the presence and assistance of counsel attaches the moment a police investigation focuses on an accused. The police must warn an accused person of his right to remain silent and his right to the presence of a lawyer.

Many constitutional lawyers and those active in legal-aid work believe the day is not far off when all the states will be required to furnish counsel to indigent persons for every type of offense. More criminal appeals to the Supreme Court in recent years have been based on the claim of lack of counsel than on any other basis for appeal.

(7) *Trial by jury.* Although not considered a fundamental right, the notion of a jury trial must have been very basic to due process, or else the Constitution, an essentially succinct document, would not deal with it in some detail in Article III, Section 2, and again in the Sixth Amendment, where it states, ". . . in all criminal prosecutions, the accused shall enjoy the right to a speedy and public trial, by an impartial jury of the State and district wherein the crime shall have been committed . . ." [33]

(8) *Right to call witnesses and confront adverse witnesses through cross-examination.* There is an abiding mistrust of the secret informer in Anglo-American jurisprudence, an abhorrence of anonymous accusations and the accusatory rumor. This would seem to apply only to criminal trials and does not always exist in administrative proceedings or the grand jury.

(9) *Right to an impartial judge.*

(10) *Right to an impartial prosecutor,* who will serve the accused as well as the state.

(11) *A presumption of innocence* of the accused person until proved guilty beyond a "reasonable doubt." The state has the burden of proof, not the defendant.

(12) *Prohibitions against cruel and unusual punishments.*[34]

(13) *Right to reasonable bail.* This feature of criminal justice has special cogency because so many persons processed in the criminal court are poor.

THE DISSONANCE OF PRINCIPLES AND PRACTICE

The ideals of due process when translated into procedural regularities, as we have seen, are calculated to redress the disparate balance between an accused person and his accusers. Granted that we have developed the most libertarian rules of criminal justice of any nation. Nevertheless, the rules themselves do not actually define or limit the operations of the police, the prosecution, and the courts, who are responsible for their enforcement. These agencies rework the rules for organizationally prescribed ends which are consistent with values of efficiency, high production, and maximizing individual careers. The formal rules of due process generate a state of tension between due process ideals and practice. One of the major functions of formal organization or bureaucracy is to reduce the uncertainties of the environment. The rules of due process introduce elements of chance into the organizational environments of the enforcement agencies. "Bureaucratic due process" represents the "practice" which they have devised to reduce the elements of chance in their respective work milieus.

The rules of due process, as expanded and strengthened by the Supreme Court, are predicated on the existence of an adversary system of criminal justice. The rules envision a "combative" procedural system wherein prosecution and defense (who are admittedly possessed of unequal resources) will clash. After the dust has settled, the data which determine guilt or innocence will have emerged. Unfortunately, this model of criminal justice does not exist in fact. At each stage of the process a tacit but erroneous assumption is made. It is assumed that the accused will ultimately have "his day in court." Oversights, mistakes of judgment, and the capricious behavior of enforcement officials will be carefully reviewed—by the next higher authority. The sort of individualization necessitated by due process introduces special complications in the daily work of the enforcement agencies, interfering with organizational values of efficiency and maximum production. As a result, all the screening agencies in the system of criminal justice move a case along toward a trial—which seldom occurs.

Police officials, the prosecution, and grand juries provide little real protection for accused persons because of the rather superficial standards of proof of guilt they require in order to move a case along to the next step in the criminal screening process.[35] Although prosecution agencies are bound by arrest standards of "probable cause" in connection with felonies (a reasonable belief that a crime has been committed and that the accused is the perpetrator), pressures of administrative efficiency too often resolve any doubts in favor of the organization. Police see little danger in this practice because they feel that any legal or factual irregularities will be unearthed in the trial court (the mansion). But as a practical matter there is widespread resentment among police of judges and courts, which they think seek to "handcuff" them through stricter rules of due process. Police "efficiency" is thereby threatened, and as a consequence strategies of evasion of rules are perfected which tend to support the validity of a given arrest and charge. "Probable cause" as an arrest standard is at best not necessarily enough evidence to charge a defendant. But prosecutors are too often ready, because of their own organizational requirements, to prosecute. Grand juries, through their indictment power, become too readily the willing handmaidens of a system of justice which has been called by Jerome Skolnick a system of "justice without trial."

Under these circumstances of mass administration of criminal justice, presumptions necessarily run to regularity and administrative efficiency. The negation of the presumption of innocence permeates the entire system of justice without trial. All involved in the system, the defense attorneys and judges, as well as the prosecutors and policemen, operate according to a working presumption of the guilt of persons accused of crime. As accused after accused is processed through the system, participants are prone to develop a routinized callousness, akin to the absence of emotional involvement characterizing the physician's attitude toward illness and disease. That the accused is entitled to counsel is an accepted part of the system, but this guarantee implies no specific affirmation of "adversariness" in an interactional sense. Indeed, the most respected attorneys, prosecuting and defense alike, are those who can "reasonably" see eye to eye in a system where most defendants are guilty of some crime.[36]

In a recent study of the guilty plea practices in the United States, it was estimated that when all pleas to both felonies and misdemeanors are combined, the total guilty plea convictions rate may be almost 95 per cent. When felony cases alone are used as the basis for the calculation of guilty pleas, the total is estimated to be 70 to 85 per cent.[37] In another study, sponsored by the American Bar Foundation, of a representative sample of counties in all fifty states, the median percentage of guilty pleas in felony cases was 69 during the year studied, 1962.[38] Conclusions drawn from the foregoing data are in general affirmed by the data drawn from Metropolitan Court over a period of fifteen years, from 1950 to 1964 inclusive, at the felony level.

The following table shows the total number of accused persons who pleaded guilty in a given calendar year without completing the formal process of a trial, and the total number of cases processed or disposed of during the given year, expressed in absolute terms and as a percentage relationship. By "processed or disposed of" is meant all those persons who were either convicted by plea or trial, dismissed, or acquitted—in other words, concluded cases awaiting formal sentence.

While the American Bar Foundation data include many cases of individuals who were not represented by counsel, *every* accused person in the Metropolitan Court data was furnished counsel either privately or through an elaborate legal-aid defender system. Nevertheless, the results over a fifteen-year period indicate a consistently high conviction rate by way of plea before trial—consider-

Table 1: Volume of cases pleading guilty before trial in Metropolitan Court
(1950–1964)

Year	Cases processed	Pleaded without formal trial	Per cent pleading guilty
1950	2498	2287	91.55
1951	2905	2666	91.77
1952	3220	3034	94.22
1953	3390	3185	93.95
1954	3762	3436	91.33
1955	3391	3190	94.07
1956	3140	2859	91.05
1957	3356	3130	93.26
1958	3926	3692	94.04
1959	3923	3732	95.13
1960	4639	4416	95.19
1961	4002	3785	94.58
1962	4363	4070	93.28
1963	4953	4616	93.19
1964	5030	4673	92.90

ably higher than the aforementioned national median rate of 69 per cent.

An even more definitive omen of the administrative, non-adversary character of "bureaucratic due process" is expressed in the table on page 30, in which the same years are examined. The universe with which we begin each calendar year is the total number of persons indicted by grand jury. Since so much attention and regard is lavished upon the institution of trial by jury as a procedural safeguard in our system of jurisprudence, the data take on added significance and meaning.[39]

Of course, although the actual criminal process does not reflect the textbook version of a trial (there being so few actual trials), the system is not in imminent danger of collapse. Nor have the participants withdrawn sentiments supporting its legitimacy. Further, we are *not* suggesting that many of those who plead guilty

Table 2: Volume of cases disposed of by trial in Metropolitan Court (1950–1964)

Year	Indictments found by grand jury	Total cases disposed of by trial	Per cent disposed of by trial
1950	2676	113	4.22
1951	3217	137	4.25
1952	3638	127	3.49
1953	3532	131	3.70
1954	3934	112	2.84
1955	3235	102	3.15
1956	3159	114	3.60
1957	3524	115	3.26
1958	3772	107	2.83
1959	4314	104	2.41
1960	4750	116	2.44
1961	4319	142	3.28
1962	4392	162	3.68
1963	4997	150	3.00
1964	5073	145	2.85

are innocent of any crime. Quite the contrary is true in all probability, and in many instances those who have been able to negotiate a lesser plea have done so willingly, even eagerly, in order to obtain the benefits of a more favorable disposition. Indeed, *the system of justice by negotiation, without trial, probably tends to serve better the interests and requirements of the guilty.* As compensation for his acquiescence and participation, having observed the prescriptive etiquette in compliance with what is expected of the defendant, he is rewarded. But an innocent person is confronted with the same role prescriptions, organizational features, and structural alternatives, with few of the accompanying possibilities of assuagement.

The central fact is that accused persons shun jury trials and prefer to alleviate the onerous burdens of their defendant status through a negotiated lesser plea. To risk a jury trial poses an obviously great statistical probability of conviction, often of far more serious charges than those administratively available in the bargained-for plea. The threat of a jury trial is one of the subtleties employed by the prosecution to reduce a defendant's resistance. Jury trials are discouraged in any event, because they are time consuming, expensive, and introduce an altogether cumbersome dimension into a system which is otherwise characterized by regularity, supreme rationality, and efficiency. Indeed, at the time of sentence, whether one was convicted after a trial or by way of a plea becomes a basis for invidious comparison. Prosecution and defense will often stress, by way of mitigation for the accused, that he has not caused the state to go to the expense of a time-consuming trial. The defendant who has been convicted after trial receives rather less generous treatment than one who has negotiated.

It would appear at least tentatively that once one is caught up in the system as an accused (indicted) individual, there is little chance of escaping conviction. This is so whether one pleads guilty or actually proceeds with a trial. As the results in Table 3 indicate, the jury trial conviction rate is also quite formidable.

Disagreements which resulted in hung juries and therefore produced no disposition are not included in the total cases disposed of by trial. Thus, for example, in 1950 there were actually 128 trials, but only 113 resulted in an actual disposition of a case.

One social critic expresses the view, probably shared by many, that the criminal court in America is "inefficient, corrupt, and archaic." [40] While these appellations have a somewhat value-laden character, to call the court system "inefficient" may be inaccurate. It seems to have articulated structures of a highly "rational" character, calculated to achieve maximum production and near maximum rates of conviction. If these are the ends to be pursued, then the criminal court is highly "efficient."

Table 3: Conviction rates in cases disposed of by trial in Metropolitan Court
(1950–1964)

Year	Total cases disposed of by trial	Convictions, number and per cent		Acquittals	Dis-agreements (hung juries)
1950	113	92	(81.41)	21	15
1951	137	103	(75.18)	34	12
1952	127	95	(74.80)	32	22
1953	131	101	(77.09)	30	18
1954	112	88	(78.57)	24	8
1955	102	82	(80.39)	20	7
1956	114	94	(82.45)	20	11
1957	115	81	(70.43)	34	8
1958	107	90	(84.11)	17	8
1959	104	96	(92.30)	8	21
1960	116	104	(89.65)	12	6
1961	142	127	(89.43)	15	9
1962	162	142	(87.65)	20	8
1963	150	127	(84.66)	17	6
1964	145	123	(84.82)	14	8

THE ROLE OF IDEOLOGY

How then can the court's functionaries and the clients it serves continue to defend as legitimate such a negatively evaluated, oppressive social arrangement? Partly the answer lies in the concept of ideology—the fact that "man does not live by bread alone," that he must seek to develop an ideology to justify, reinforce, and give meaning to interests he pursues. These ideologies and their elaborate rationales become as real and consequential as the material interests. Every regime, in all epochs, involving varied groups and political systems, has sought to claim legitimacy by employing "political myths" or "formulas." The "divine right of kings"; *"liberté, égalité, fraternité";* "justice under law"; "due process"; "all men are created equal"—these are prominent examples of the political myth. Ideologies need not be and often are not the weapons of a conspiracy of rulers to keep the ruled submerged or to falsify a given state of affairs. On the contrary, they are often nurtured and subscribed to by all strata, rulers and ruled alike, to resolve the inevitable discordancies and incompatibilities of belief systems and behavior or action systems.

One ideological aspect of due process, as we have seen, is the concealment of the emergence of justice without trial, the system of justice by negotiation. Another and probably more significant aspect of the ideological rationale which makes the criminal court palatable to all involved is the almost universal belief on the part of accusers and accused alike in two other basic suppositions:

(1) A defendant in a criminal court is really beaten by the deprivations and limitations imposed by his social class, race, and ethnicity. These in turn preclude such services as bail, legal counsel, psychiatric services, expert witnesses, and investigatory assistance. In essence, the concomitants of poverty are responsible for the fact that due process sometimes produces greatly disparate results in an ill-matched struggle.[41] Further, if these disabilities of the accused were alleviated, then the traditional principles of due process would function to make "justice" available to all. Due process is revered and believed in as the normatively established, time-honored means for obtaining justice, but its lack of vitality is explained away by sociological inequities.

Largely ignored in this argument is the institutional structure— the organizational characteristics and requirements of the criminal court itself. It mediates between the rules as they have been elaborated and the accused person, who has been presented to the court for disposition by still other organizational structures— the police and the district attorney.

The organizational variable affects the values and ideals of normatively established procedures of due process and produces outcomes other than those intended. The *élan vital* of the organization itself has a thrust, purpose, and direction of its own, at

variance too often with the stated values of due process. We can tentatively state at least seven elements in the organizational variable which tend to deflect it from its prescribed goals:

(a) Occupational and career commitments and drives generate priorities which have a higher claim than the stated organizational goals.

(b) Empire building.

(c) Organizational goals of maximum production, which in their implementation are inconsistent with due process and rule of law.

(d) Institutionalized evasions of due process requirements.

(e) A routine of idiosyncratic and deviant solutions—which are denied on an overt level—to organizational problems of production.

(f) Secrecy and relative immunity from scrutiny.

(g) Individual pathology meeting its needs and finding its satisfactions while cloaked in organizational authority and under cover of the activities of the organization.

(2) The second basic ideological rationale which supports the legitimacy of the criminal court is the ameliorative-therapeutic model of the court, the origin of which is to be found in the Positivist school of criminology and serves to cast the criminal in the role of a "sick" person. The court then becomes something more than a legal structure; it is also a clinical way station in the long process of individualization of "treatment" of offenders.[42]

For judges, lawyers, probation personnel, and accused persons, the psychiatrist not only has a place in the court setting but tends to validate legal judgments in terms of medical "science." In fact, psychiatry becomes the theology by which legal procedures and pronouncements are interpreted and their legitimacy reinforced for all of the foregoing categories of persons, the accusers and the accused alike. In addition, the charismatic quality of the various occupational roles, even as routinized in the court setting, tends to overwhelm the court's clients, who continue to believe sufficiently in the efficacy, justification, and intentions of psychiatry, probation, and law as "helping" disciplines.

Positivist criminology simply rejects a legal definition of crime and postulates the idea that "punishment" should be replaced by "scientific treatment" of crime. Almost from its inception as a special discipline in medicine, psychiatry has had a role in the administration of the criminal law. As psychiatry developed its theories and made contributions to the study of human behavior, especially in the deviant and the criminal, it also became more powerful socially and politically. Psychiatry has greatly affected the ideas of those who deal with offenders administratively in courts and prisons—as well as in the more remote sphere of human organization in the corporation, shop, factory, and office. Every bureaucracy now has a psychiatric practitioner on tap to deal with the maverick or cantankerous employee—or for that matter anyone—who appears to have "gotten out of line."

But the connection between psychiatry and the court's ameliorative-therapeutic concept is best understood in terms of psychiatry's objectives. Basic to psychiatry as an intellectual effort is its attempt to understand the nature of human behavior and its development, and to control its direction and purpose by manipulating the individual and his environment. Psychiatry, through research and evaluation, claims to develop indices of predictability about human conduct, making possible controlled results for the greater felicity of man and society. But instead, psychiatry, through what one of its most distinguished practitioners in the criminal courts has termed its "psychoauthoritarianism," [43] has become in many instances a *threat* to offenders, because psychiatrists are called upon to participate in virtually every stage of a criminal proceeding. As a consequence, that which another prominent authority in the field, in an unflattering comparison with wire tapping, has termed "mind tapping," [44] is employed without the consent or cooperation of the accused. The practical effect is often to deprive him of certain elements of due process, including the privilege against self-incrimination or ultimately even the right to a trial. For once a psychiatrist has determined that a person is "mentally ill" or "sick" and unable to stand trial, he is more than likely to spend a much longer time behind bars in a mental hospital than if he had been simply convicted of a crime in the first place.[45]

Despite strong evidence (the data are now fairly overwhelming) that "criminals" and "delinquents" do not possess personality characteristics significantly different from the rest of the population, and that the prevalence of psychoses, neuroses, and other disturbances among them is not significantly different from similarly matched samples of the rest of the population, psychiatrists still exert an extremely strong influence in the criminal courts.[46] Because of their ideological utility and the charismatic character of their profession, they are simply too useful to dispense with in the administration of the criminal law.

The nosologies, the jargon, and the values of psychiatry, as they are embodied in the ameliorative-therapeutic model which is used in the criminal court, help to disguise and falsify the reality of what occurs. The most analogous situation is the custodial-mental hospital setting, where what is for all practical purposes a prison, presents a therapeutic façade.

The heart of the matter, however, is that in its relationship with other institutions, publics, and its clients, the court uses the language of therapy to justify such varied phenomena as the juvenile court, the indeterminate sentence, the sexual offender laws and civil commitment of the mentally ill, and the use of psychiatric reports before guilt or innocence is determined. Even judges speak the language when imposing sentence.

In practice, measures and techniques that tend to deprive a person of liberty under the guise of an exercise in therapeutic method are seen as punishment, and psychiatry has been seriously criticized on that account. The most strenuous objectors have indicated, in effect, that psychiatry has lent itself to questionable enterprises, and its affirmations of helping through punishment virtually amounts to the discipline being unable to perceive the real nature of its role.[47]

Metropolitan Court has in fact reached the ideal-typical goal in personnel and structure. In its arrangements for bail, counsel, and elaborate psychiatric and probation services, it represents what all who have had serious concern with the criminal court have hoped for. But the court which serves as the universe of this case study produces an administrative result in which the overwhelming majority of defendants simply plead guilty. The idealized version of due process is not translated into social action. The administrative instruments and resources are co-opted in behalf of the court organization to deal more effectively with a large caseload of defendants, by processing them toward a guilty plea.

An observer of the Soviet legal system has called the Soviet criminal trial "an appeal from the pre-trial investigation." In the Soviet Union the "trial" is simply a recapitulation of the data collected by the pre-trial investigator. Notions of a trial being a "tabula rasa" and presumptions of innocence are wholly alien to Soviet notions of justice. How closely does "bureaucratic due process" and its accompanying non-adversary system pose a discomforting parallel to the Soviet system, wherein "the closer the investigation resembles the finished script, the better. . ."? [48]

3

The criminal court as organization and communication system

> ". . . Pelting petty officer . . .
> Dress'd in a little brief authority,—
> Most ignorant of what he's most assured,
> Plays such fantastic tricks before high heaven
> As make the angels weep; . . ."
> —William Shakespeare, *Measure for Measure*

The fastening of the label "criminal" upon an individual, even by virtue of information that may be fragmentary in all respects, is a major institutional enterprise.

> The screening device which sifts . . . the person's overall performance . . . is a very important instrument of social control. We know very little about the properties of this screen, but we do know that it takes many factors into account which are not directly related to the deviant act itself: it is sensitive to the suspect's social class, his past record as an offender, the amount of remorse he manages to convey, and many similar concerns

which take hold in the shifting moods of the community. This
may not be so obvious when the screen is dealing with extreme
forms of deviance like serious crimes, but in the day-by-day
filtering processes which take place throughout the community
this feature is easily observable. Some men who drink too much
are called alcoholics and others are not, some men who act oddly
are committed to hospitals and others are not, some men who
have no visible means of support are hauled into court and others
are not—and the difference between those who earn a deviant
label and those who go their own way in peace depends almost
entirely on the way in which the community sifts out and codes
the many details of behavior to which it is witness. In this respect, the community screen may be a more relevant subject for
sociological research than the actual behavior which is filtered
through it.[1]

The criminal court is that part of the "community screen" which
sifts out and labels the accused person. Metropolitan Court, the
subject of this case study, is probably one of the largest criminal
courts in the world in terms of number of cases processed each
year and personnel engaged in the enterprise. It is the highest court
of original criminal jurisdiction in one of the largest cities in America, empowered to deal with all serious offenses known as felonies,
and with lesser crimes.

The defendant population of Metropolitan Court is drawn
largely from the lower socio-economic strata—the usual pattern in
a criminal court. Minority groups tend to be over-represented, including Negroes, but not nearly to the extent that they are in national data. Virtually every major ethnic group in the United
States is represented to some extent, although skin color continues
to be a critical factor in one's vulnerability.

It is interesting that "white collar" criminals do not appear to
have the extensive immunity to prosecution that sociologists have
believed. During 1964 the court's probation division investigated
3,643 persons; of these approximately 8 per cent, by virtue of

their education, occupation, income, and nature of their offense, would qualify as "white collar" criminals. While these offenders might ultimately have fared better by plea or sentence, they could not by virtue of a more favorable social position overcome the organizational mechanism of the court entirely—contrary to a rather shopworn notion among criminologists. In addition, the probation division collected more than $250,000 in restitution money during that year, a substantial amount of that sum being amounts returned to their victims by "white collar" offenders.

Metropolitan Court has been in existence since colonial days and has an annual operating budget in excess of $3 million. Salaries of its nine judges are among the highest in the world, averaging $35,000 a year. An elaborate court staff is at the judges' disposal, including a chief clerk and assistants and deputies performing all sorts of functions from clerical duties to that of court crier, wardens of the grand jury, court reporters, and court attendants. The attendants are armed and "protect" the physical environment of the courtroom. There are also many stenographers, typists, and interpreters. Each judge has in his personal entourage a law assistant, a confidential attendant, and a law secretary or clerk. The secretaries fill patronage positions, for the judge himself is of course very much a political figure, being elected for a term of years. Lately, in the city where Metropolitan Court is located, both major parties have entered into arrangements where certain judicial candidates run unopposed as part of a political "swap."

The other patronage jobs are the chief clerk and certain other clerical positions. Almost all of the lower-level positions in the court structure are filled through civil service, but any of these personnel are of course available to a judge for tasks which may be beyond their ordinary duties. For example, a civil service attendant, because of his political activity or even his special skills, may be asked to perform more prestigious and less onerous duties.

The nine justices constitute a board of judges who, in addition to their judicial functions in the courtroom, have administrative responsibility and overall control of the major activities of the court. There are three major court functions, each with its own staff of professionals and clerical, service personnel. One is fundamental case record keeping and processing, which is the function of the clerk of the court and his staff of assistant and deputy clerks, interpreters, stenographers, and court attendants. This office also furnishes interpreting, stenography, typing, and policing services for the entire court. Some few members of the clerk's office, as previously indicated, may augment the personal staffs of retainers assigned to each judge. The word "retainers" is used deliberately, because the judge's personal staff has many of the qualities of organization and personal fealty that characterized the feudal lord and his staff of retainers. The relationship is one of extreme deference and fierce loyalty based not so much on any charismatic quality of the judge but rather on the largesse and privileges he bestows and dispenses. This feature sets the judge's personal entourage apart from the ordinary court staff.

The "clerk," of course, is not necessarily an unskilled, low-paid menial. Many clerks in the clerk's office are lawyers who perform the various ministerial and record processing tasks that are critical to the functioning of the court. Many have substantial local political party clubhouse ties, even though they have attained their positions through civil service promotions. In this almost all-male world in the clerk's office, the entering rank is that of court attendant; the line of promotion leads to deputy and assistant clerk positions paying in excess of $16,000 a year. The chief clerk and his assistant, as political appointees, receive considerably higher salaries. The usual profusion of typists and stenographers, mainly female, are relatively low-paid civil service personnel.

The second important segment of the court structure is the probation division. This unit is headed by a chief, his two deputies, and an administrative assistant, who are responsible for a staff of supervisors and approximately sixty probation officers. The probation division also has its own clerical services—some fifty typists, clerks, statisticians, stenographers, and receptionists. Again, most of the personnel, except for the typing and clerical staff, are males.

The third court segment, the psychiatric clinic, employs five psychiatrists, two of whom are employed on a per diem or part-time basis. There are also a number of clinical psychologists whose function is largely diagnostic testing. The clinic also has at its disposal a major public psychiatric hospital with all its resources for special tests and such periods of observation as may be required. And the clinic has its own filing, clerical, and stenographic personnel and facilities.

Physically quartered in the same building but not part of the court budget or having any formal and *direct* administrative relationship with the court, is a legal aid defender service. It is largely privately endowed and employs a staff of fifteen to eighteen full-time lawyers. This unit has its own quarters in the building and maintains a clerical staff and other supportive services with its own budget. Its function is to provide legal services to persons arraigned in Metropolitan Court who are unable to retain private counsel for a fee. The city in which Metropolitan Court is located pays part of the budgetary requirements of this legal service, and in this sense the agency is no longer a private legal aid service but is more in the nature of a "public defender" service for those of limited financial means. Thus, unlike most of the rest of the nation prior to the *Gideon vs. Wainwright* decision requiring counsel in all felony cases, no person who appears in Metropolitan Court is ever without the assistance of a lawyer at every stage of his case.

During 1964 this legal defense unit acted as counsel for approximately 70 per cent of the Metropolitan Court case load. There is no formal administrative connection between the unit and the court, but the service plays a vital function in the court's daily operations and in realizing its organizational goals. As a consequence, there is really a close, continuing liaison between the defender service and all court officials from the judge down to even the most minor functionary.

Also quartered in the court building is the office of the district attorney, which has its own budget and personnel. This office has direct formal and informal relations with the court structure and the legal aid unit, for it is the source of the court's business. While specific organizational features and characteristics of the office of the district attorney are beyond the scope of this book, one significant aspect of its organization must at least be mentioned so that we may understand how it affects the larger court through which it funnels its cases.

After decades of unsavory and corrupt practices at the county and municipal level in the city in which Metropolitan Court is located, there was concerted public pressure to remove certain municipal and county offices from the political patronage system. Both major political parties, anxious to avoid scandal and to improve at least superficially the tarnished image of municipal government, agreed to sponsor joint candidates for some judicial and prosecutor posts. Qualities of personal integrity, honesty, intellectual achievement, and dedication to public service were to be the ideal characteristics of potential candidates, regardless of party label.

As a result, the office of the district attorney has in the past twenty-five years taken on the character of a civil service post. The chief prosecutor has always enjoyed the political endorsement of both major parties and, in furtherance of the public service image, has recruited assistant district attorneys from among the graduates of leading law schools. There are still a number of patronage people in the office and even civil service personnel with strong clubhouse ties. Indeed, many of the bright young men recruited from the better law schools usually seek political affiliation to further their careers in the office or afterward, in private practice or some other post, in or out of government. But in the main, politics is much less a part of the district attorney's office than it once was.

The office employs a full-time staff of approximately seventy assistant district attorneys. Six bureau heads are responsible for the major activities of the office, and they supervise the daily work of the assistants who in turn file a brief report on each plea of guilty accepted, proposed, or negotiated. Each case must be accounted for as a unit of production. At the annual office banquet, it is customary for the district attorney to praise his staff in glowing terms, especially for their "batting average," which is an omnipresent standard of performance.

Most assistants remain in the office from three to five years until they make a "connection" or some other appropriate step upward in the career line. Usually it is the "failures" who remain behind to become bureau heads in the office or assume other supervisory functions. As a result the office takes on a more rational-impersonal orientation, geared to aggressive prosecution without "fear or favor." This is not to say that political concerns and pressures are not present. But they have in large measure been concealed by an impartial civil servant organization and a public service image, which is vigorous in maximizing production to justify its budget, and which does not as readily lend itself to informal political considerations at the beck and call of the "political club."

The assistant district attorneys operate within the confines of office policy enforced by bureau heads. Not only must the total output of cases be maximized, but the "batting average" must reflect the kind of superior efficiency supposedly present in the impartial, public-service type of district attorney's office. This perception of the office contrasts to the old-fashioned "political" model based on patronage with its personal and informal commitments, now for the most part rejected. Of course, the office of the district attorney still retains the traditional ideology that its function is not simply to prosecute but more important to "protect the innocent" and to exercise great care and prudence in its decisions to prosecute. The public prosecutor has a unique role in our system of jurisprudence. He is required to be "impartial" in the sense that he must try to determine whether the accused is really guilty of the crime charged. He must not only use facts unfavorable to an accused but must also not conceal facts favorable to him. The stated measure of success is not the number of convictions but their "fairness." Thus the district attorney is not an ordinary party to a criminal controversy but has a higher standard, an impartial concern with "fairness" and "justice." As a practical matter, however, prosecutors have great discretion and power to use their office for idiosyncratic, non-organizational ends, or to use it in a manner that overrides obligations to the accused in order to meet unstated requirements of the organization.[2]

As a practical matter, self-imposed organizational pressures, such as getting the most for each prosecution dollar and demonstrating the superiority of the public-service model of the office, direct all energies toward maximum production. The new type of assistant district attorney is far less politically connected and is wholly dependent upon his superiors for their employment recommendations when he moves on—whether to another political office or to private practice. As in any other bureaucratic setting, the rewards are dispensed only to those who have "played the game" and have conformed to the expectancies of their superiors.

The criterion of office efficiency becomes the number of convictions (or pleas) produced, which in turn are built and based upon the growth of impersonal, rational procedures which energize and amplify bureaucratic structures. Max Weber has written:

> The more bureaucracy is "dehumanized," the more completely it succeeds in eliminating from official business love, hatred, and all purely personal, irrational elements which escape calculation. This is the specific nature of bureaucracy and it is appraised as its special virtue.[3]

In reality, therefore, an accused is, so to speak, ground between the millstones of the district attorney and of the court. Both have their respective organizational requirements of maximum production.

Figure 1, on the next page, depicts some of the structural relationships in the system.

Note that counsel, whether privately retained or of the legal aid variety, have close and continuing relations with the prosecuting office and the court itself. Indeed, lines of communication, influence, and contact with those offices, as well as with the other subsidiary divisions of the office of the clerk and the probation division and with the press, are essential to the practice of criminal law. Accused persons come and go in the court system, but the structure and its personnel remain to carry on their respective career, occupational, and organizational enterprises. The individual stridencies, tensions, and conflicts which certain cases may generate within the system are overcome, because the relations of all the groups in the court setting require it. They must preserve their own relations and interaction at all costs.

In some modern bureaucratic settings, the organization appears to exist to serve the needs of its personnel rather than its clients.[4] The client becomes a secondary figure in the court system as in other large organizational settings. He is a means to other, larger ends of the organization's incumbents. He may present doubts, contingencies, and pressures which challenge or disrupt existing informal networks, but they are usually resolved in favor of the organization. Even the accused's lawyer has far greater professional, economic, intellectual, and other ties to the various elements of the court system than to his own client. Yet the lawyer is the only member of the system who is officially recognized as having a special status and obligations. He is an "officer of the court," and he is expected to maintain a standard of ethical performance and duty to his client, as well as to the court, which is far higher than that expected of ordinary individuals occupying the various occupational statuses in the court community.

One other aspect of organizational structure must be considered

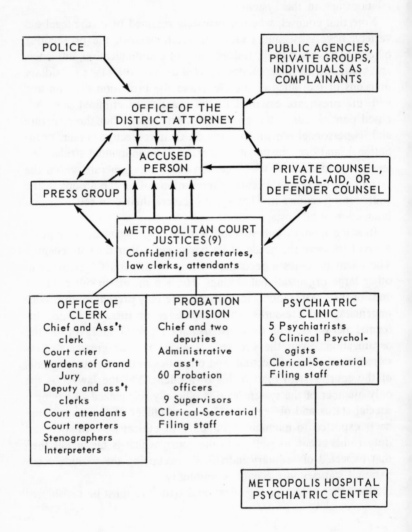

FIGURE 1: SOME STRUCTURAL RELATIONSHIPS IN THE
METROPOLITAN COURT ORGANIZATION

POLICE

PUBLIC AGENCIES,
PRIVATE GROUPS,
INDIVIDUALS AS
COMPLAINANTS

OFFICE OF THE
DISTRICT ATTORNEY

ACCUSED
PERSON

PRESS GROUP

PRIVATE COUNSEL,
LEGAL-AID, OR
DEFENDER COUNSEL

METROPOLITAN COURT
JUSTICES (9)
Confidential secretaries,
law clerks, attendants

OFFICE OF
CLERK
Chief and Ass't
clerk
Court crier
Wardens of Grand
Jury
Deputy and ass't
clerks
Court attendants
Court reporters
Stenographers
Interpreters

PROBATION
DIVISION
Chief and two
deputies
Administrative
ass't
60 Probation
officers
9 Supervisors
Clerical-Secretarial
Filing staff

PSYCHIATRIC
CLINIC
5 Psychiatrists
6 Clinical Psychol-
ogists
Clerical-Secretarial
Filing staff

METROPOLIS HOSPITAL
PSYCHIATRIC CENTER

in attempting to measure a social reality such as the "closed community" of a court. And the essence of this aspect of the problem has been captured by Aaron Cicourel:

> Most of the data that sociologists honor as "given" .`. . . are largely the product of bureaucratically organized activities, for example census bureaus, vital statistics bureaus, correctional agencies, welfare agencies, and business agencies. The multitudinous perceptions and interpretations that went into the assembly of such data are invariably lost to the reader or user of such materials. The quantitative features must be accepted by fiat. The fact that even factual data are subject to perceptions and interpretations which may vary with the actor's biography, the occasion of recording, the explicit or implicit rules employed for deciding the sense of the objects or events categorized, and the stated language and unstated meanings which were relevant to the particular observer, means that these are variables to consider in assessing the relevance and importance of such data.[5]

Every public agency or privately owned corporation interprets its past, present, and future operations through the medium of the annual, semi-annual, or quarterly report. Sometimes an elaborate affair with color plates, intricate charts, and impressive tables, it is essentially a brief for the agency or corporation. In effect it advises the publics concerned that the operation is in good hands and merits confidence. It is the "official" window through which the author-agency wishes to present itself. It is an important vehicle of justification for public or private funds already spent and requested for expanding future budgets.

In the case of a public agency, the "report" justifies its budget. In essence it says, "Look, how busy we are!" Figures on how many cases were processed or clients served are usually accurate, as are most of the other innocuous items in the report of Metropolitan Court and similar courts. Any organization, public or private, whose flow of funds depends largely upon production data as evidence of its efficiency and social utility, will find it hard to resist pressures to tamper with the figures. It is a basic fact of bureaucratic life that production and production figures are a fetish. Nothing demolishes criticism faster than a robust set of production figures which reflect an ever onward and upward increase, and they are therefore almost blindly worshiped. Reports may be slanted, certain data may be highlighted or "puffed up" to meet felt needs for additional budget and staff, but reports of public agencies usually reveal nothing of social consequence about the real organizational world they come from.

An agency's published data are of course never adequate or appropriate for the sociologist, except as a point of beginning. Sociological perspective involves a process of "seeing through" the façades of social structures. The official data are an organizational curtain to be drawn aside so that the important network of human activities may be laid bare. For all the personnel of Metropolitan Court—judges, lawyers, down to the most menial clerk—the fact that more than 90 per cent of its clients plead guilty each year rather than stand trial arouses no curiosity, interest, or surprise. In fact, it is never mentioned. It is a "world taken for granted." It is statistical evidence of the agency's high efficiency in giving the public maximum service for each tax dollar spent. In similar fashion, the police and prosecution seek "successful" cases as grist for their respective enforcement and production "mills," in part to justify their budgets and in part as ego-satisfying evidence of workmanship and professional expertise. Thus the policeman seeks the "good pinch" [6] and the prosecutor the "airtight case."

THE SIEVE EFFECT

Each enforcement agency seeks to maximize its viability with a set of "successful" prosecution figures. Nevertheless, it is an interesting study in contrasts to observe the incredible statistical difference between the number of crimes committed or reported and the number of persons actually dealt with officially in the law enforcement machinery. Criminal and delinquent activity has a rather small overall liability of being subjected to official action—that is, of the offender being detected, apprehended, and convicted. The FBI reports on a rather consistent basis that only about 25 per cent of all crimes reported are actually cleared by arrest.[7]

The police have wide powers of discretion in selecting persons for processing. Similarly, prosecutors may choose to ignore offenses or to prosecute, and grand juries and courts of preliminary hearing are also engaged in a selection-sifting process of some kind. There is therefore a sieve effect in the criminal process, and it is directly relevant to the organizational analysis of one of the most important elements in the whole process—the court.

Some aspects of the preliminary sifting of potential accused clients have already been discussed. We have not noted that a fundamental characteristic of the sieve effect is that initially its escape holes are somewhat broad and coarse. They begin to sift in an increasingly finite manner as we move structurally from the initial point of police handling to the court of preliminary hearing, then to the arena of the criminal court where felonies are tried. There the process almost freezes, and only infrequently from then on can the accused free himself from the procedural engine in which he is enmeshed. It is as though he had been, in social-psychological terms, prepared and shaped for his ultimate disposition and presented to the court in a crude fashion for final processing. In these final steps the accused person is helped to redefine and restructure his concept of "presumed to be innocent" to that of a "guilty" person. Figure 2, on the next page, examines in cursory fashion the gross possibilities as they may terminate at any point in the processing of a felony case, either in being "sifted" to the next step or in freedom.[8]

The virtual freezing of the sifting process occurs in phases IV and V of Figure 2, when a maximum of organizational structure, personnel, and skill are brought to bear upon the individual.

Table 4 confirms our contention that once the case of an accused

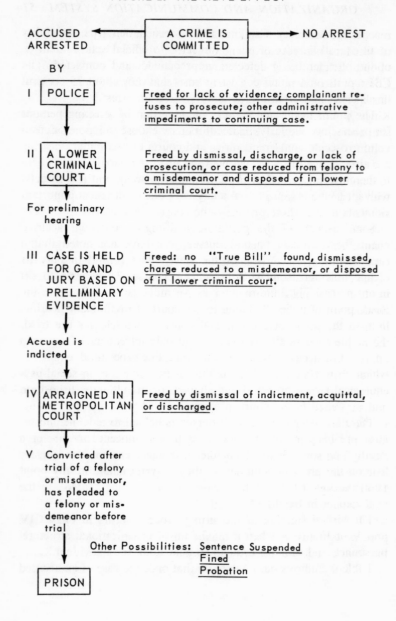

FIGURE 2: THE SIEVE EFFECT

ACCUSED
ARRESTED ◄──────── A CRIME IS ────────► NO ARREST
                    COMMITTED
BY

I   POLICE   Freed for lack of evidence; complainant re-
                        fuses to prosecute; other administrative
                        impediments to continuing case.

II A LOWER   Freed by dismissal, discharge, or lack of
    CRIMINAL   prosecution, or case reduced from felony to
    COURT   a misdemeanor and disposed of in lower
                        criminal court.
For preliminary
hearing

III CASE IS HELD   Freed: no "True Bill" found, dismissed,
    FOR GRAND   charge reduced to a misdemeanor, or disposed
    JURY BASED ON   of in lower criminal court.
    PRELIMINARY
    EVIDENCE

Accused is
indicted

IV ARRAIGNED IN   Freed by dismissal of indictment, acquittal,
    METROPOLITAN   or discharged.
    COURT

V   Convicted after
    trial of a felony
    or misdemeanor,
    has pleaded to
    a felony or mis-
    demeanor before
    trial

            Other Possibilities: Sentence Suspended
                                  Fined
                                  Probation

PRISON

reaches the Metropolitan Court level in his "career," the possibility of freedom becomes problematic, if not slight. These data draw upon a different geographic universe (the Kings County Criminal Court of Brooklyn, New York), but deal with a population similar in size and composition to that of Metropolitan Court. The Kings County court also has many structural and procedural similarities, as well as similarities in case load composition and volume, which would make for a valid comparison.

Justice Sobel of the court, who collected the data, did so largely to demonstrate that relatively few persons who are initially charged with a crime are indeed found to have committed the original version of the crime charged. It is a not uncommon administrative device of the police to couch the original version of their charge against an accused in the most extreme form possible within the confines of a given set of facts. Thus, very often, an original charge of felonious assault (with a weapon) is reduced at the initial hearing to a more realistic one of simple assault, or even to disorderly conduct. In part, this is the sort of activity to which Sobel refers in his data, but he also empirically spells out the wide disparity in the number accused and those actually ultimately convicted in our courts. Also to be noted is the manner in which the situation becomes firm after one is indicted and begins his processing in a court dealing with felonies, such as the Brooklyn court or Metropolitan Court.

The data are given in the form of round numbers and approximate percentages. The format has been altered slightly to promote clarity, and some of the "stages" of the data have been relabeled. The figures all refer to adult felony arrests in cases for the years 1960 through 1962.[9]

Two almost casual observations can be made about Table 4 which further support the concept of a diminution in the sifting process as a case reaches the level of indictment and beyond. Of the total of ten thousand persons indicted by the grand jury (item 8), 8,740 either pleaded guilty or were adjudged or convicted

Table 4: Disposition of adult felony arrests, Kings County (1960–1962)

Stage of proceeding	Number of cases	Per cent of total	Per cent remaining
1. Preliminary arraignment in a lower criminal court	32,000	100	100
2. Discharged, dismissed on technical or procedural grounds or otherwise adjusted at preliminary arraignment	2,000	6.2	93.8
3. Dismissed on merits (case was not proven) at preliminary arraignment	6,000	18.6	75.2
4. Reduced to misdemeanor charge at preliminary arraignment	12,000	37.6	37.6
5. Held for grand jury	12,000	37.6	37.6
6. Dismissed by grand jury	1,000	3.1	34.5
7. Charge reduced by grand jury to a misdemeanor	1,000	3.1	31.4
8. Indicted by grand jury	10,000	31.4	31.4
9. Indictments dismissed for procedural reasons as defective	320	1.0	30.4
10. Indictments dismissed on facts and law of case	640	2.0	28.4
11. Adjudged youthful offender	860	2.6	25.8
12. Pleas before trial to a felony	3,200	10.0	15.8
13. Pleas before trial to a misdemeanor	4,280	13.4	2.4
14. Convicted after trial of a felony	350	1.2	1.3
15. Convicted after trial of a misdemeanor	50	.3	1.0
16. Acquitted	300	1.0	0.0

after trial (total of items 11 through 15), or approximately 87 per cent of all those ultimately indicted. This approximate figure is not significantly different from the Metropolitan Court figures for 1950–1964, which were of course precise figures and not rounded off as are the data in Table 4.

The sieve effect is the result of the increase in personnel and the greater intricacy of structure brought to bear on the accused as he moves toward and into the court for the felony trial itself.

INSTRUMENTS AND PRESSURES PROMOTING PLEAS OF GUILTY

During the course of Anglo-American history, convicted persons have sometimes been burned at the stake, drawn and quartered, or pressed to death (also known as *peine forte et dure*). This last mode of execution was an excruciating style of death employed especially in cases where an individual refused to plead guilty or not guilty to an indictment.[10] Nothing so appalling or violent has been used in the contemporary administration of criminal law. But the basic overriding concern is still with a *plea,* rather than anything more elaborate, by way of disposing of a criminal case. The methodology employed to get that plea has undergone the kind of subtle refinement and elaboration that only the modern features of formal organization can provide.

The fundamental event which places an accused upon the horns of a dilemma, leading to his ultimate desire for a negotiated or bargained lesser plea, is very simply the decline of the jury system. Whatever that system's merits or drawbacks may be, the fact is that defendants shun a jury trial.[11] This is borne out by the Metropolitan Court data in Table 3, attesting to the dearth of jury trials in that court. But an even more critical factor for the individual accused is his knowledge (whether he senses it intuitively or has learned it from his jail companions or his lawyer) that juries are notoriously prone to convict. In simple terms, the outcome of any jury trial often turns upon the question of whom the jury will be-lieve—the assertions of the police, law enforcement officials and their witnesses, or the accused. The answer forthcoming with frequent regularity is: the police and those offering testimony in their behalf. This fact lies at the root of an accused's reluctance to risk a jury trial and in part accounts for the consequent decline of the jury as an important feature of the system.

An accused is confronted with a formidable barrier at the very outset of his passage as an indicted person (Table 4, stage 8), in that he is perceived as a far more serious offender than if he had been sifted out at an earlier stage in his career. The charges he now faces are those of a felony. This fact alone helps to determine the kinds of pressures he will face and how the staff of Metropolitan Court will react to his processing. And, at the outset, the accused's position is complicated by still another factor which dissuades him from braving the possible consequences of a trial by jury—the multiple-count indictment.

An indictment is a list of criminal charges. Its purpose is to notify an accused of the precise nature of his alleged offenses so that he may prepare a defense. But a law violation which occurs through a single act can legally result in one being charged with several offenses. A typical indictment for, let us say, possession of more than an eighth of an ounce of heroin, will read as follows:

Count #1. Felonious possession of a narcotic drug.

Count #2. Felonious possession of a narcotic drug with intent to sell.

Count #3. Unlawfully possessing a narcotic drug.

A quite common indictment for burglary may read:

Count #1. Burglary 3rd degree.

Count #2. Possession of burglar's instruments.

Count #3. Unlawful entry of a building.

Or one for armed robbery:

Count #1. Robbery 1st degree.

Count #2. Assault 2nd degree.
Count #3. Assault 3rd degree.
Count #4. Grand larceny 1st degree.
Count #5. Carrying a dangerous weapon.
Count #6. Petit larceny.

Another quite common illustration of the force and effectiveness of the multiple-count indictment occurs in connection with so-called "white collar" offenses. Modern commercial transactions and enterprises have been so rationalized that they are conducted largely with letters of credit, notes, checks, elaborate records, securities, mortgages, bonds, stocks, certificates, and other documents. These of course are subject to theft, forgery, manipulation, and fraud. It is therefore not uncommon for a case of embezzlement or theft based on a series of forgeries to result in an indictment containing more than a hundred counts of forgery, grand larceny, and other charges of theft and fraud. Each count is grounded upon an individual document connected with a particular person who used it in the course of his thefts. The pressure on the accused to seek some sort of compromise of all these charges becomes intense, to say the least. Conviction by a jury on all counts could result in an accused spending the rest of his life in prison.

There are, therefore, depending on the alleged facts in each case, many combinations available which result in an accused being charged with multiple felonies and lesser misdemeanors growing out of the same event. Using the Robbery 1st degree indictment as an example, if an accused were to "gamble" and proceed to a jury trial, it is quite possible (indeed, probable) that he could be convicted on each and every count of the indictment and face many years in prison if the sentences were fixed to run consecutively instead of concurrently on each count. In some states the Robbery 1st degree count *alone* would warrant a sentence of up to thirty years. But typically in Metropolitan Court, if an accused has had no prior record and if he has capably performed the defendant role, he probably will receive a lesser plea of, let us say, a misdemeanor such as simple assault or petit larceny.

The impulse to seek a negotiated plea at this point, in view of the dire possibilities of going to trial and losing, is almost impossible for an accused to overcome. The "benefits" and advantages of a lighter sentence for a lesser plea, or even the possibility of a suspended sentence, become overwhelmingly attractive. For example, as subsequent data will indicate, the possibilities of a defendant being placed on probation are far greater if he has pleaded to a lesser offense, rather than having been convicted after a trial. An accused's fears of harsh treatment if he does not plead are hardly groundless, considering what courts and judges do to defendants who remain recalcitrant and go to trial.

The jury system and the multiple indictment, then, are used as the initial blows to further collapse an accused's will to resist at this phase of his processing. The district attorney is the moving force, the upper of the millstones, as we have indicated, between which the defendant is ground. The prosecutor calls all the strategic plays:

(1) He decides when the case will appear on the calendar for any particular stage of the proceeding.

(2) He recommends the amount of bail, if any is to be granted (although final discretion is up to the judge).

(3) He selects the particular term or part—that is, which judge will hear or try the case.

(4) He has virtually complete discretion as to whether to prosecute and on what legal grounds (of course, subject to restriction of law).

(5) He often determines what lesser plea, if any, will be accepted in lieu of the case going to trial.[12]

This last prerogative is the most important weapon in the prosecutor's arsenal, for it furnishes his basis for power in negotiations with the significant "others" in the court. The district attorney is the one court figure most aggressively interested in obtaining a negotiated plea rather than a case culminating in a combative trial. First, there is the almost impossible administrative task of going through the elaborate procedures of a court trial for each case. The personnel and other resources of the prosecutor's office simply could not carry such an impossible burden. And the prosecutor would lose a degree of dominance over those variables essential to the maintenance of his "public image" and the "batting average." In those cases which end in a plea, the prosecutor usually retains a far greater influence over the ultimate sentence or disposition. Indeed, the very plea which is finally negotiated and accepted by the accuser and the accused fairly well defines the limits of punishment ultimately involved.

But even the civil-service model prosecutor is subject to political and bureaucratic pressures of important "others." He is himself observed by the police, judges, lawyers, and lesser officials in the court community, such as those who administer the short-term prison housing for persons awaiting disposition of their cases. This last is a frequently overlooked element of internal pressure in the court system. Accused who are not released on bail are housed in the short-term prison; as a rule it is overpopulated in terms of its capacity. Each day a statistical resumé of the jail population is sent to the prosecutor, the judges, and the probation division. Its message is not lost upon its recipients: faster production.

The short-term prison attached to Metropolitan Court was built to house approximately nine hundred males. The average population awaiting disposition there is double that number and often far more. The conditions at the prison, even if improved, would still be onerous in view of the overcrowding. At times, bail practices become a function of the extent of crowding in the short-term prison. The prison is used in still another way, namely, to further soften defendants reluctant to plead. In short, crowded conditions in the short-term prison become an extremely functional adjunct for the total administrative process of the court system.

The external pressures on the prosecutor depicted in Figure 3

FIGURE 3: PROXIMATE AND MORE REMOTE PRESSURES
ON THE PROSECUTOR

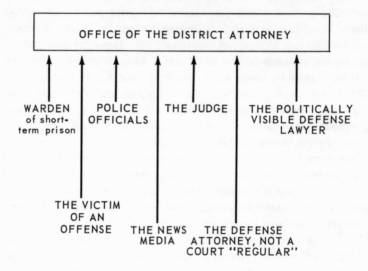

are set out in terms of intensity and proximity of the pressures they exert. Of greater intensity and proximity are those of the short-term prison population (a substantial part of the case load), as represented by the warden of that institution. Police officials and personnel who are moved by pressures and demands of their own organization for production, are a second important source of pressure on the district attorney for production results, as are the judges. Politically visible defense lawyers, unlike attorneys who appear only casually and irregularly in Metropolitan Court and who have therefore failed to develop political or informal relationships with the district attorney, must be accommodated somehow or at least extended certain courtesies.

More remote, and exerting presures of less immediate intensity, are the victims of offenses committed by accused persons, the news media, and the defense attorney who is not part of the intimate circle of official persons who make up the tight-knit, xenophobic community of the court. Victims who may be seeking restitution, the return of stolen property, or just revenge or retaliation are a constant source of minor harassment, but they are easily put off or somehow pacified. The news media and those attorneys who are not "regulars" are dealt with on a quid pro quo basis of "favors" given and returned, and while they exert pressure, their placation is not insurmountable.

On the other hand, of more intimate concern to the prosecutor are pressures from those with whom he lives in a virtually symbiotic professional relationship in order to maintain his own organizational equilibrium. Thus, although the prosecutor has many powers and prerogatives, and possesses the initiative at virtually all times, he nevertheless depends upon the close, continuing help of the police, judges, lawyers, and other lesser functionaries to attain his ends. And they in turn depend upon him for the identical objectives they desire, namely, as few trials as possible.

Besides the time, energy, and resources that the court organization is reluctant to expend on trials, as a bureaucracy it is loath to engage in activity whose predictability it is unable to control. The rational component of formal organization avoids the fortuitous, the random, and the contingent, such as a jury trial. Greater faith is placed upon symbiotic relationships and structured expectancies to meet the individual and group needs of the court participants, rather than a working through of legal abstractions such as due process. The deviant or even maverick individual who predicates his official conduct solely on accepted notions of due process, or chooses possibilities of action which run counter to normatively established routines, is quickly isolated, neutralized, or re-socialized.

Professionals of the older variety (for example, lawyers) or of the "new" professions (for example, social workers, probation officers, psychologists), have increasingly become part of an occupational mass known as a "salariat," employed and seeking employment in large-scale organizations.[13] This development has created conflict between the professionally oriented individual who seeks satisfaction and recognition outside the immediate, narrow confines of his organization, and the specific task requirements of his organization. Two types of professionals emerge: the "cosmopolitan" seeks satisfaction and recognition outside the organization; the "local" perfects his relationships and rituals within the organization. The "local" develops a method of organizational maneuver, promoting at all times his idiosyncratic career interests but at the same time showing a seemingly passionate, loyal concern for the organization. His "career" rises or falls with the organization, in contrast to the "cosmopolitan," whose interests range beyond the organization—even though he may be just as zealously concerned with career escalation.

Even though the organizational world of the court—which is in many respects unique—contains an ongoing struggle between a legal due process perception and an ameliorative-therapeutic perception of the court's function, these are overridden by the superordinate requirements of efficiency and production. The usual staff-line struggles of quality versus quantity, the divergent concerns, professional commitments and interests, occupational goals, values, and perspectives of those engaged in the enterprise are overcome, harnessed, and coordinated into a working consensus to alter effectively the accused's view of himself as "presumed to be innocent."

Individuals with a professional orientation or worldly concerns are considered deviants and are not tolerated if they are discovered invoking other than ritualized organization means and objectives. The standard of performance, the model of commitment and loyalty becomes the "local"—the bureaucratically oriented routineer. Because the individual in organizational society is so dependent upon the various bureaucratic enclaves for material goods and services, he is motivated to conform to their expectancies and demands.

Individuals are thereby motivated to "play the game" rather than deviate. (The court organization, as we shall see later, invokes still other controls and motivations for compliance by group members.)

Those professionals in the court, such as probation officers, psychologists, and psychiatrists, who believe they will manipulate the legal structures in line with their orientations, discover too late that they are mere instruments to be utilized for larger organizational ends. They find that their body of professional skills cannot be autonomously employed but must be exercised within the framework of precise organizational limits and objectives.

THE "MORAL CAREER" OF AN ACCUSED PERSON

We have described the journey of an accused person through the sifting process of the court system as a "career." Sociologists use the term not necessarily to describe conventional notions of occupational careers but to delineate the social-psychological steps in transition from one status to another.[14] Erving Goffman speaks of "the moral aspects of career—that is, the regular sequence of changes that career entails in the person's self and in his framework of imagery for judging himself and others."[15] Goffman elaborates:

> The moral career of a person of a given social category involves a standard sequence of changes in his way of conceiving of selves, including, importantly, his own. . . . Each moral career, and behind this, each self, occurs within the confines of an institutional system, whether a social establishment such as a mental hospital or a complex of personal and professional relationships. The self, then, can be seen as something that resides in the arrangements prevailing in a social system for its members. The self in this sense is not a property of the person to whom it is attributed, but dwells rather in the pattern of social control that is

exerted in connection with the person by himself and those around him. This special kind of institutional arrangement does not so much support the self as constitute it.[16]

One can apply Goffman's analysis to the case of the accused person who moves from civilian to criminal, or is convicted. We begin with a complainant, who may be a private individual, a policeman, the district attorney, or an administrative agency. If the gravamen of his complaint is sustained in a lower criminal court of first instance, the individual complained of has become an accused person. Henceforth the accused will be dealt with and processed by a variety of mediators and agencies who will relay him along. But already he has marked the first milestone in his career—he has become an accused person.

He may now face an assistant district attorney who will point to the multiple counts of an indictment and ask whether the accused would rather go to trial than plead to some proposed lesser offense. Even the most obtuse accused will understand the full import of this.

To police administrations, a plea of guilty is a welcome addition to the statistical evidence of their effectiveness, for they correlate a favorable public image and a high conviction rate. Equally important is the fact that valuable police time that would be spent in trial testimony is freed for other activities.

Much police work at every level—federal, state, and local—is conducted on the basis of information furnished by informers and paid agents. Because of the nature of this mode of operation, which encroaches on dearly held ethical values, police work and negotiation with other agencies is best carried on in relative secrecy. Thus the kind of informal negotiations which are conducted by police, district attorney, defense counsel, and judge in connection with a negotiated plea are best performed in virtual secrecy. In bargaining with an accused, the police use the possibility of a negotiated plea as leverage, usually to get further information. Of course, at times they are completely out of bounds in their zeal, making offers of immunity or threats of punishment wholly beyond their authority or function.

The vested interest of the district attorney and the police, and their role as agents, is readily perceived and understood by an accused person. He will have sensed certain negative attitudes toward police and will have internalized them long before he has ever been arrested. The agent-mediator roles of judges, lawyers, probation officers, psychiatrists, and members of his own family are not so easily understood. The accused could reasonably define them as allies.

But some of the same reasons which serve as the basis for the district attorney's actions apply also to the judge. According to the ideology of the law, the judge is required to be not only impartial but active in seeking out and preserving the rights of all offenders. Nevertheless, he also has a vested interest in a high rate of negotiated pleas. He shares the prosecutor's earnest desire to avoid the time consuming, expensive, unpredictable snares and pitfalls of an adversary trial. He sees an impossible backlog of cases, with their mounting delays, as possible public evidence of his "inefficiency" and failure. The defendant's plea of guilty enables the judge to engage in a social-psychological fantasy—the accused becomes an already repentant individual who has "learned his lesson" and deserves lenient treatment. Indeed, as previously indicated, many judges give a less severe sentence to a defendant who has negotiated a plea than to one who has been convicted of the same offense after a trial.[17]

The lawyer, whether a public defender or a privately retained defense counsel, is subject to pressures peculiar to his role and organizational obligations. But ultimately he is also concerned with strategies leading to a plea. Again, impersonal elements prevail—the economics of time, labor, expense, and the commitment of the defense counsel to the rationalistic values of the court organization; the accused who expects a personal, affective relationship with his lawyer is likely to be disappointed. The lawyer "regulars" of Metropolitan Court are frequently former staff members of the prosecutor's office. They utilize the charisma, "know-how," and contacts of their former affiliation as part of their stock in trade. An accused and his kin, as well as others outside the court community, are unable to comprehend the nature and dimensions of the close relations between the lawyer "regular" and his former colleagues in the prosecutor's office. Their continuing colleagueship is based on real professional and organizational needs of a quid pro quo, which goes beyond the limits of an accommodation one might ordinarily expect in a seemingly adversary relationship. Indeed, adversary features are for the most part muted and exist in their attenuated form largely for external consumption. The principals—lawyer and assistant district attorney—rely upon each other's cooperation for their continued professional existence, and so the bargaining between them usually is "reasonable" rather than fierce.

In his relations with his counsel, the accused begins to experience his first sense of "betrayal." He had already sensed or known that police and district attorneys were adversaries, and perhaps even a judge might be cast in such a role, but he is wholly unprepared for his counsel's performance as an agent or mediator.

It is even less likely to occur to an accused that members of his own family may become agents of the court system. Upon the urging of other agents or mediators, relatives may believe they are really helping an accused negotiate the best possible arrangement under the circumstances. Usually the lawyer will activate next of kin in this role, his ostensible motive being to arrange for his fee. But soon counsel will suggest that they appeal to the accused to "help himself" by pleading. Gemeinschaft sentiments are to this extent exploited by a defense lawyer (or even at times by a district attorney) to achieve specific secular ends, to conclude the matter with all possible dispatch.

Sooner or later the probation officer becomes an agent in an accused's processing, depending upon when his services are invoked by judicial requisition. In his role as an agent-mediator there is a fundamental theme—the professional self-conception of a "case worker in an authoritative setting." Probation officers and psychiatrists in the court must, according to established procedures, accept as a "given" the facts of a defendant's case as they are presented by the police and the district attorney. This has specific consequences in their relations with an accused. In other words, they view important aspects of a defendant's social biography in terms and meanings defined for them by agents hostile to the accused. Thus they see him, whether before or after he has pleaded, as already "in treatment."

The accused is usually unable to understand that he does not enjoy the worker-client or doctor-patient relationship with these functionaries. On the contrary, their professional services are preempted by the court organization, and they tend to impute primacy to the organization for the content and meaning of their roles. Usually, a defendant speaks much more freely and reveals a good deal more about himself to psychiatrists and probation officers than he would to other agent-mediators. But he can also reveal too much; he overlooks the lack of real confidentiality present in his relationship with them, and this too has consequences in terms of his ultimate disposition. The court organization may rely heavily on probation and psychiatric reports, especially in those cases where there are no other firm or compelling legal, political, personal, or other criteria to use as a basis for disposing of a case. Bear in mind that the justifications and rationales employed by these agents are grounded in a stock of knowledge about the accused that is pre-cast by police and prosecutor, whose objectivity may be problematic. So, to a large extent, probation and psychiatric reports reaffirm and recirculate the same knowledge about the accused originally furnished by police and prosecutor—refurbished in the patois and argot of social work and psychiatry.

The probation officer has an important function as an agent-mediator, especially after the accused has pleaded and has begun to have second thoughts about the matter. This function may be best described as "cooling the mark out." The phrase was originally used to describe that part of a confidence game in which the operatives leave one of their number behind to discourage the victim from going to the police and to help him accept his new social situation. The victim of, let us say, a swindle must be furnished with a set of apologia or rationales so that he can redefine himself in suitable and defensible terms, instead of going to the police to complain. His embarrassment and defeat are assuaged by the operative who is "cooling him." In similar fashion, in other social matrices, losers and defeated persons must be somehow "cooled out" in order to avoid some sort of social explosion. Erving Goffman furnishes an illustration in which one spouse "decourts" another by maneuvering the marital partner into a divorce without incurring undue hostility. Or in the case of a dying person, the cooling role is assumed by a doctor or priest.[18] Helping an accused person to accept defeat is another aspect of the agent-mediator role which is thus of great significance. The lawyer, probation officer, psychiatrist, and next of kin perform important "cooling out" functions. Even the police, prosecutor, and judge may occasionally find it necessary to perform such a function as an accused is processed toward a reconceptualization of self, in the course of changing his initial plea of "not guilty" to one attesting guilt.

We have previously noted that the short-term jail which houses defendants awaiting disposition is frequently crowded to double the intended capacity. Although this is a state of affairs not deliberately created, the discomforts occasioned thereby are employed as a weapon against the accused by the prosecutor and judge. A recalcitrant accused can be socialized relatively quickly by an extended sojourn in the remand jail, including setting bail at a level high enough so that he cannot meet it. The common refrain heard in the remand jail, from those who have been there for an extended period, is a desire to plead quickly and get sentenced, so that they can be moved to a more commodious prison. The greatly crowded conditions, while unintended and unforeseen, are used as part of the process of reducing an accused's resistance to the various agent-mediators.

While it is true that efforts have been made to simplify and develop less onerous bail procedures,[19] most defendants are still subject to the usual difficulties connected therewith. The bail or jail feature of the system is not the crucial one in terms of an accused's defeat; it is only one feature in the total array of structure and personnel in the prosecutor's arsenal of weapons.

Although many accused persons are never confronted with the problem, their alleged wrongdoing being unsung in the press, there are instances in which the news media serve in an agent-mediator role. Obviously this is not their intention, for they desire to serve publics and ends of their own. But it is virtually impossible for an accused to receive a fair trial by "an impartial jury," should he elect to do so, because an "impartial jury" could never be constituted if the press, radio, and television have established for weeks in advance of his "trial" that a defendant is guilty.

In summary, the accused is confronted by definitions of himself which reflect the various worlds of the agent-mediators—yet are consistent for the most part in their negative evaluation of him. The agent-mediators have seized upon a wholly unflattering aspect of his biography to reinterpret his entire personality and justify their present attitude and conduct toward him. Even an individual with considerable personal and economic resources has great difficulty resisting pressures to redefine himself under these circumstances. For the ordinary accused of modest personal, economic, and social resources, the group pressures and definitions of himself are simply too much to bear. He willingly complies with the demands of agent-mediators, who in turn will help "cool him out."

Figure 4, on the next page, does not spell out the interrelationships of the various agent-mediators, but it depicts the accused's ultimate situation. Of course, he does not initially assume that all these pressures are allied against him.

FIGURE 4: THE ACCUSED VIS-À-VIS HIS AGENT MEDIATORS

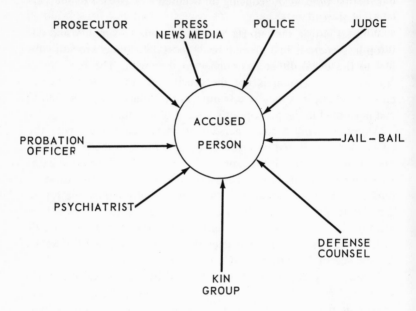

One of the major requisites of due process is a "public trial," but justice by negotiation avoids public scrutiny. Technically, it may meet the minimum requirements of due process (the defendant having waived jury trial), but whether it meets the ideological and historical criteria of due process is at least an open question.

The court, unlike most other formal organizations, functions as a genuinely "closed community" in that it successfully conceals the true nature of its routine operations from the view of outsiders— and sometimes even from some of the participants themselves. It socializes its members and participants toward compliance with specific objectives which are not part of the official goals of justice and due process.

But the usual organizational use of ideological goals and internal discipline are inadequate in the court situation. They must be augmented and implemented. In dealing with this problem the court is unique in a number of respects, and the organizational solutions that have been elaborated are calculated to overcome not only the resistance of the accused but the possible reluctance and work alienation of his accusers.

4

Discipline and perspective in the criminal court

> "It is horrible to think that the world could one day be filled with nothing but those little cogs, little men clinging to little jobs and striving towards bigger ones . . . men who need order and nothing but order . . ."
>
> —Max Weber

Every organization tries to achieve its ends through the rational employment of its structure and personnel. Just as social values can be separated into real and stated values, so organizational goals can be similarly described. In a broad sense they furnish a convenient set of definitions of purpose, a set of perspectives and ideological recipes, to which one can refer in structuring one's organizational conduct. In that sense, organizational goals can effectively discipline a group of different individuals, endowing them with a uniform set of perspectives in the service of the organization.

Institutions such as a criminal court, which possess historical and other claims to legitimacy, have great difficulty reinterpreting and readjusting their traditional tasks and goals when new demands are imposed by social change. In the case of a criminal court the official or stated goals remain the same, because these represent a constitutional, ideological, and historic "given." But how are priorities *really* assigned to various activities, and what personnel and resources do those activities command? Amitai Etzioni elaborates the notion behind this question:

> The researcher will define as the *real* goals of the organization those future states toward which a majority of the organization's means and the major organizational commitments of the participants are directed, and which, in cases of conflict with goals which are stated but command a few resources, have clear priority. Sometimes, establishing intimate contact with key participants allows the researcher to determine how aware informants are of any discrepancy between real and stated goals. Generally, however, it is unwise to depend entirely on interviews for information on an organization's real goals. An examination of the allocation of resources and direction of efforts is often a necessary complementary research method for obtaining satisfactory results.[1]

If the systematic study of life in modern society is indeed a study of organizations, then the identification of organizational goals is crucial. Whether official or real, goals furnish meaning to human existence. But in the legal realm, in particular, efforts to separate the apparent from the real are often met with charges of "cynicism" or "muckraking." A criminal court's stated organizational goals may be couched in terms of "justice" and "rule of law," but its organizational instruments and resources are committed to priorities of efficiency and production.

An organization's goals are grounded in the values of its environment. It is constantly redefining its relationship with its environment and is alert to shifting moods—for example, changes in markets, population, technology, and production methods. In response to structural and value changes in the environment, an organization may alter its goals or completely displace them. It may execute a complete about-face in functions, methods, goals, and purpose; but having made those necessary situational adjustments, it will survive, although greatly altered in character and purpose.[2]

Organizational goals call for the development of instruments for the attainment of those goals. And instruments have a tendency to generate "needs" of their own which must be catered to; they have a way of sidetracking the organization from original goals or ends. Thus, in a private, voluntary, fund-raising organization, specific goals generate a set of instrumental means and personnel for the attainment of those goals—and the instruments in turn generate a set of built-in needs. When the original fund-raising goals disappear or become obsolete, the original activities of fund-raising will continue to meet the needs of an already existing instrument, albeit for a new goal or end. The March of Dimes is a perfect illustration. When the relief of poliomyelitis became obsolete because of the Salk vaccine, the organizational structure and personnel, as "instruments," possessed a viability and thrust of their own; they continued the activity by substituting a new goal of research in arthritis and birth defects.[3] The social implications of this kind of transformation in an organization may seem modest or even innocuous, but on other levels of human activity, in other times and places, means which become ends can prove disastrous for society.

The kinds of values that produced due process and other Western notions of justice have been superseded. While the stated goals of the criminal court may still appear to be the same—at least as ritual affirmations—the instrumental structures used to achieve those goals are not. In fact, the evidence indicates that fundamental changes in values and accompanying changes in instruments in an industrial-urban society have so altered one another that virtually all that remains of the original criminal court goals are its ideological affirmations.

Two other elements affect organizational goals, particularly as they apply to the criminal court: organizational environment and organizational co-optation. First, the organization must appear to be performing a valuable, necessary service or function. It needs permanent social support to compete with other agencies for public funds. So the organization keeps its ear to the ground in an effort to discern changes that may modify its budget downward. And it deliberately overestimates budgetary requirements or looks for new projects. This is an essential element of the "empire building" feature of bureaucracy.[4]

Co-optation is the assimilation of competing power structures which threaten the organization. These new elements may force the organization to modify its original goals. Philip Selznick, in his study of the Tennessee Valley Authority, furnishes an illustration of this feature in his description of the way in which persons and interests actually hostile to some of the goals of TVA were admitted to its management. As a result, the new elements shaped TVA goals in terms of their own interests, modifying and altering original objectives.[5] The somewhat comparable situation in the criminal court is the co-optation of social work in the form of probation services. And at an earlier stage in the Anglo-American history of criminal law administration, psychiatry was co-opted. In both cases, of course, the co-optation was part of a larger development—the ideological transformation of the criminal law, from the classicist emphasis on deterrence and punishment to positivist notions of rehabilitation and reformation through individualization of offenders. Nevertheless, the organizational structures of the legal institutions had at least initially to recognize psychiatry's claims in the area of determining criminal responsibility by admitting its practitioners to the courtrooms.

RATIONALISM AND THE EMERGENCE OF MASS SOCIETY

The official goals of an organization are not difficult to determine in most instances. They are stated in corporate charters, advertising slogans, or prefaces to annual reports, or even on company or agency stationery. In the case of Metropolitan Court, as with certain other public agencies, they are engraved on the building façades:

EQUAL AND EXACT JUSTICE TO ALL MEN OF WHATEVER STATE
OR PERSUASION

GOOD FAITH IS THE FOUNDATION OF JUSTICE

THE ONLY TRUE PRINCIPLE OF HUMANITY IS JUSTICE

JUSTICE IS DENIED NO ONE

IMPARTIALITY IS THE LIFE OF JUSTICE AS JUSTICE IS OF GOOD
GOVERNMENT

EVERY PLACE IS SAFE TO HIM WHO LIVES IN JUSTICE

ONLY THE JUST MAN ENJOYS PEACE OF MIND

WHERE LAW ENDS THERE TYRANNY BEGINS

One need not have a sophisticated knowledge of the historical roots of these mottoes to discern the goals of the organization or the presumed values underlying them.

It is commonly assumed that the basis for due process and rule of law in Western jurisprudence rests on the Magna Carta of 1215. But their real origin is in the Old and New Testaments,[6] and in a social era whose life style has little resemblance or relevance to modern mass societies. Somehow we assume that our values, including due process, have maintained their relative order of importance regardless of the passage of time and the shift in Western society from an emphasis on kinship and status relations to the impersonal, secular, rational modes and instruments of social organization. Lawyers and judges still speak, perhaps naively, of "immutable principles" when they talk about justice and due process. When virtually every other aspect of human existence has been touched and modified by mass society and its precursors of secularism and rationalism, they find it difficult to recognize that their universe of discourse has also been affected.

The official goals of the criminal court, based on ancient values, remain; due process, justice, and rule of law are necessary ideologies. But concerns of secularism and rationality, based on modern values of efficiency, maximum production, and career enhancement, have deflected and perhaps displaced those goals. So there is also a new angle of vision more harmoniously in accord with the rationalization of justice. These perspectives are organizationally geared through bureaucratic discipline to mesh with the new goals. The impersonal relations inherent in this kind of social structure produce accusers and accused possessed of a self which is ideal for organizational purposes—one which is vulnerable to manipulation and capable of manipulating others.

BUREAUCRATIC AUTHORITY IN THE CRIMINAL COURT

In the criminal court, agent-mediators who manipulate others in the course of their work roles are themselves subject to manipulation. This is a form of bureaucratic authority different from the usual criteria of Max Weber and others, and it includes several component variations of Weber's rational-legal authority:

(1) Manipulation as a supervisory device

(2) Obedience apart from deference for "rules" and "office"

(3) Authority by complicity

(4) The panopticon effect

Together with the organizational goals, these constitute a system of internal discipline and a uniform set of perspectives for everyone in the organization. Because almost every participant in the criminal court will at some time question the validity, purpose, and rectitude of the near-total defeat of accused persons, a variety of controls, organizational disciplines, and perspectives have been developed to keep everyone fairly well socialized and in line with organizational needs and demands.

Two relatively recent works in the field of formal organization indicate the dimension of manipulation as an element of bureaucratic authority. Morris Janowitz, discussing the impact of changing technology upon internal organizational relations in the military establishment, writes:

> The morale and coordination of a complex group of specialists cannot be guaranteed simply by authoritarian discipline . . . the impact of technology has forced a shift in the practices of military authority. Military authority must shift from reliance on practices based on *domination* to a wider utilization of *manipulation*. Traditional or ascriptive authority relies heavily on domination, while manipulation is more appropriate for authority based on achievement. By domination we mean influencing a person's behavior without reference to the goals sought. Domination involves threats and negative sanctions rather than positive incentives. It tends to produce mechanical compliance. Manipulation involves influencing an individual's behavior less by giving explicit instructions and more by indirect techniques of group persuasion and by an emphasis on group goals. While the term "manipulation" has come to be thought of as morally reprehensible, it describes the efforts of leadership when orders are issued and the reasons for them are given. It is impossible to analyze modern institutions without reference to a concept such as manipulation, or some more socially acceptable equivalent. Manipulation involves positive incentives rather than physical threats; manipulation does retain the threat of exclusion from the group as a control.[7]

The second illustration involving the use of manipulation as an aspect of bureaucratic authority draws upon a wholly different universe—the social case work agency. Peter Blau and Richard Scott write:

> In certain types of service organizations, such as casework agencies and mental hospitals, pseudo democracy often takes the form of a therapy-oriented or psychiatric approach to supervision. In this approach the subordinate is not blamed for imperfections in his performance or for failing to conform to directives; instead, his behavior is analyzed to detect what unconscious forces have led to his resistance. This practice was observed to occur frequently in the weekly supervisor-worker conferences in the wel-

fare agencies, where the worker would bring his difficult cases for discussion. The supervisor would aid him in solving the technical questions involved in determining client eligibility, would help him to understand the behavior of his client, and sometimes would indicate to the worker how his own feelings and needs were influencing his relation with the client. Accordingly, the workers often found themselves rather than the clients to be the subjects of these discussions—so much so that there were many references among workers to the supervisory practice of "caseworking the worker." There were, of course, sometimes legitimate grounds for subjecting the worker's feelings and behavior to critical analysis—to help him refrain from projecting his own needs and interests into his casework relations . . .

However, the psychiatric approach to supervision in social work is subject to abuse. What is conceived to be a very democratic method of supervision—not blaming subordinates but helping them understand their problems—turns easily into a manipulative controlling device. When there were differences of opinion between the supervisor and the caseworker on how to deal with certain problems of a client, the supervisor was tempted to analyze the worker's motives for disagreeing rather than to demonstrate why his judgment was better in terms of professional or other objective standards. Workers whose judgment frequently differed from that of their supervisor might be accused of being "unable to accept supervision." The practice of questioning the workers' unconscious motives tended to elevate the superordinate into an omniscient power. Workers found that they could not be right in any disagreement since their arguments were not accepted at face value but dismissed as being rationalizations to mask unconscious resistance. Subordinates are defenseless against this criticism because the very act of questioning it "proves it right." [8]

We have quoted extensively, because Blau's observations have direct relevancy and application to the criminal court. This kind of manipulation is used to control the work perceptions and routines not only of probation officers, who see themselves as "case workers," but of other personnel as well. The minor official or civil servant in the court setting is constantly kept off balance; he assumes a continually defensive posture in the face of recurrent criticism. The probation officer is never "right" but must always give way to the superior knowledge and techniques of others who review his reports and, indeed, will rewrite them. The psychiatrist will take "guff" from almost everyone in the court structure, including orders from judges he considers to be his intellectual inferiors. His evaluations of defendants will be questioned especially when they have not "stood up" in terms of subsequent events. Lawyers are always pressured, demeaned, threatened, and downgraded by district attorneys, judges, and even probation officers—sometimes grievously, from a professional standpoint, in the presence of their client, the accused. The professional egos of all these agents are heir to continuous shocks. They are perpetually on notice that their professional skills will be utilized by the organization only on terms and under circumstances arrived at by the organization.

Operating under the guise of pseudo-democracy, the court organization utilizes manipulation to promote the myth of the court as a meeting ground of "free professionals" in the service of accused clients. The reality of the situation is that the moment organizational assumptions, directives, and goals are questioned by the "free professionals" (lawyers, psychiatrists, and probation officers), their usefulness and loyalty are simultaneously brought into question. Nothing can be more calculated to intimidate those in the court than the threat of sanctions for non-compliance or resistance. A lawyer will be denied the favors of district attorney, judge, probation officer, and others, and the collapse of his practice will be the ultimate result. Probation officers and psychiatrists will find that they too can be subjected to sanctions. The individual who questions any aspect of the validity of the organization will himself be called into question through the imputation of destructive or otherwise unpleasant motives. "Resistant to supervision," "troublemaker," "oddball," "not amenable to discipline," "disturbed mind," "unsatisfactory work habits," "doesn't recognize and respect the needs of clients or defendants"—all of these char-acterizations are utilized to minimize, downgrade, and intimidate those who question the forms of discipline or the perceptual schemes of the organization.

The judge and district attorney in the criminal court resist through legal and informal means any encroachments on their pre-rogatives, power, and authority by other professionals in the court setting. These wielders of power and authority in the court use manipulation as one of the forms of discipline and control, espe-cially toward those persons who are wont to consider themselves members of an autonomous profession.

The second variation of the rational-legal authority in the court organization is the apparent existence of a built-in obedience factor in men which makes them more tractable and submissive to organ-izational demands. We rely on two relatively recent pieces of em-pirical data as representative illustrations of the existence of this component.

In an experiment designed to test the relative viability of the "authority of knowledge" versus the "authority of office," William Evan and Morris Zelditch concluded that "almost all subjects felt obliged to obey a supervisor's decisions about administrative matters, just as they had about technical matters. Unlike the case of technical commands, however, the grounds for legitimacy also were not differentiated. . . . Subjects generally advanced 'bureau-cratic' rather than 'professional' justifications for obeying adminis-trative rules and commands. . . . Almost all subjects . . . felt ob-ligated to obey commands of their supervisor, even though for different reasons." [9]

Stanley Milgram developed empirical data on the phenomenon of obedience of far more serious implications. Briefly, Milgram's experiment involved forty persons who came from varied back-grounds in the New Haven area. They were paid a nominal sum for their assistance in a study presented to them as the effect of punishment on learning. "Punishment" was administered by means of a shock generator with thirty graded switches ranging from "Slight Shock" to "Danger: Severe Shock," and finally two switches labeled "XXX." The "victim," a confederate of the experimenter, was to act as a "learner," and the forty persons as "teachers." Every time the "learner" made a mistake, the "teacher" was told by Milgram to flip a switch increasing the shock dose in each instance. The confederate "learner" would simulate a shrieking cry of pain with each dose, but nevertheless, in twenty-six out of forty cases, upon direction from Milgram, individuals pulled every switch in increasing severity up to those last two labeled "XXX." Some subjects objected, protesting, "Oh, I can't go on with this; no, this isn't right. That guy is suffering in there. No. I don't want to go on. This is crazy." [10]

Milgram suggests that the fact that the experiment took place on the Yale University campus may have been a factor in the high rate of obedience. One group tested outside the institutional environment of Yale still showed a 50 per cent obedience rate. A similar study, conducted by Milgram, employing forty-three Yale undergraduates as subjects, produced results similar to those of the initial experiment.

Blind obedience, apart from and independent of the usual deference for "rules" and "office," appears to be an important dimension in any system of authority, including rational-legal authority. It is probably very relevant to a punitively oriented organizational setting such as the criminal court.

A third variation of rational-legal authority as it appears in the criminal court is authority by complicity. Its basis is the datum that evasion and outright breach of rules is a universal pattern for the attainment of organizational goals, which could not otherwise be achieved. [11] Heavy work volume, impossible case loads, and unrealistic work schedules exert inordinate pressures for innovation—the search for shortcuts, the use of forbidden procedures and devices, and the like—in order that production norms may be met. A well-known union leader, whose union was legally forbidden to strike, asserted that he would not have to strike to gain his ends. He would simply order his men (in this case transport workers in the New York City subways) to invoke the "book of rules." By punctiliously complying with every finite requirement of safety and prescribed procedures in the manual of rules for subway workers, they would cause an inexorable slowdown which would in effect bring all the trains to a halt as though the men had actually struck. Management everywhere is aware of the fact that the proliferation of rules, ostensibly to bring order to the affairs of an organization, has resulted in widespread violation.

But such violation is often covertly encouraged for two reasons: first, violations are often necessary to maintain production norms; second, violators become "beholden" to their superiors. In other words, there is an element of blackmail present in the supervisor-subordinate relationship, based on the shared knowledge, winked at, that the subordinate has broken rules. Authority by complicity accomplishes three ends:

(1) It promotes production.

(2) It binds the worker further into the structure of the organization.

(3) It makes him more amenable to control from within; his past indiscretions and violations, even though he had been encouraged to engage in them, are always available to be invoked against him as a supervisory weapon.

The character and nature of authority by complicity is best revealed by the experience of the "new worker" who appears in the criminal court. All organizations loathe the recruitment of new persons, because of the adjustments, difficulties, and risks involved. The new worker in the court is a threatening person, for he is un-socialized and ignorant of group norms. The probation period which many civil service organizations establish is in reality a period during which they test the mettle of the individual for conformance with official norms. Thus the new worker is always made to adhere rigidly to an onerous, exacting routine and a high standard of work performance no longer expected of other workers. It is not so much a hazing process as a sizing-up, an evaluation period during which supervisors and fellow workers decide whether the new worker can one day be admitted to the complicity of short cuts, illegal methods, and other work "secrets."

A new probation officer may be told that he must actually make the literally dozens of visits to employers, relatives, complainants, and others connected with the case of an accused to secure necessary information. The old hands "know" that if one really uses "short cuts" and inside knowledge and know-how, one need hardly ever leave one's desk and still be able to assemble a biography of a defendant adequate for virtually any court purpose. As a consequence, the new probation officer may find himself working almost twenty-four hours a day to comply with these impossible requirements. Slowly he is granted access to the inner, covert knowledge, and when it is determined that he will be kept on, he is "bound in" by being encouraged to use illegal methods and shortcuts. The new worker then becomes a genuine group member. His colleagues can breathe easier, for the new member's complicity is complete as soon as enough case records bearing mute testimony to his work "crimes" have accumulated in the files. He will then be in no position to "blow the whistle" on his colleagues and supervisors, who in any event always maintain a public stance of obeying work norms and complying with all directives and rules. One of the interesting clues to the existence of illicit modes of operation is the statement frequently made by an older worker about a contemporary who has gone on to higher supervisory rank: "He always was a faker and a phony!"

In similar fashion, other work categories in the court are bound into complicity. Court attendants who may have others "sign in" for them or otherwise falsify their actual hours, or who extend courtesies to others outside the court in return for gratuities or gifts, are common illustrations of rule violations. Lawyers may violate outright the ethics of their profession—by coercion and dishonesty in connection with the collection of a fee from a client, by acting contrary to a client's best interests in connection with a plea, or by otherwise misrepresenting facts to a client in order to gain some advantage for himself. Because the practice of criminal law, and the extent of one's practice, are so largely contingent upon the character of informal relations a lawyer develops, the lawyer's violations are largely directed against his own client in the service of his higher master, the court. Court personnel are keenly aware of the extent to which a lawyer's stock in trade involves the precarious stage management of an image which goes beyond the usual sales puff. For this reason alone, the lawyer is "bound in" to the complicity system of organization discipline.

The psychiatrist is bound in by what he knows to be the basic superficiality and perfunctoriness of most of his examinations. Ultimately, all personnel in the court, including the members of the office of the district attorney and the judge, are bound in to the system of authority by complicity because of the compelling necessity to meet the court's demanding production goals and public values by skirting the rules.

Yet, at the highest levels of the court administration the board of judges and the district attorney remain aloof and seemingly unaware of any system of complicity. They may have private knowledge, but it is never permitted to find expression even on a tacit level. Only at the middle levels of management and supervision, filtering down at the lower "field" levels, is complicity a pronounced, understood dimension for maintaining discipline. Even the accused, during the course of his career, will be bound in as he becomes in effect part of a "conspiracy" against himself.

The fourth variation of rational-legal authority in the court organization may best be described by alluding to Jeremy Bentham's scheme for a utopian penitentiary, the panopticon prison. Bentham proposed a circular building, so arranged that all the cells on the inside walls were to be visible from a central tower in the circle. An omnipresent keeper would be able to see into all the cells and observe the activities of their occupants without himself being observed by them.

We have already indicated that the criminal court is a closed community, possessed of xenophobic distrust and fear of outsiders and strangers. One might go so far as to say that the criminal court is a paranoid community. While proper objection may be raised to the use of the term, the fact remains that there are strong elements of suspicion, hostility, and resentfulness among the participants in the court's organizational community. The key phrase used over and over again by all its diverse groups is, "Cover yourself!"

Everyone in the criminal court, like the panopticon inmate, genuinely feels he is being observed at all times—and at the same time is observing others. Police, district attorneys, judges, probation officers, lawyers, and even clerks arrange their official behavior to suit the expectancies of those who will be "watching." The panopticon effect is more than the reflexive "role taking" or stage management of a performance on the level of the individual; it involves whole organizational complexes gearing their conduct and official decision-making for other organizational audiences with whom they transact business.

The district attorney will accept from an accused a plea that calls for punishment acceptable to "organizational others" who are watching—the judge, the probation division, the complainant, and even the police. Similarly, the judge will make rulings or impose sentences knowing that he is being watched—perhaps by an appellate court above him. And the probation division, in its investigations and reports, will be careful not to offend or invade the special areas of "organizational others." The panopticon effect to some extent heightens the anxiety and mistrust already present in the organization and thereby further diminishes the scope of independent decision.

The central source of authority in the court situation is the board of judges. There is never any doubt about this. The district attorney's office is the only group permitted to impinge upon judicial authority, and that by consent. Every other professional, technical, and clerical person in the court knows that he is at best "an expert on tap, not on top," subject to the judges' ultimate direction. All orders for the routine activities of the court are countersigned by a judge, whose signature makes them legal commands in the strict sense of the word. The justices cannot of course be everywhere at all times, and the variations of rational-legal authority that we have described supplement and add content and dimension to discipline.

ROLE AND PERSPECTIVE OF THE ACCUSED

The organizational structure of the criminal court also disciplines the role performance of the accused person. It gives him the stage directions of his role performance and a new set of perceptions of himself. The climax of this process in his career as an accused person occurs in the final stage of his journey—the "cop-out" ceremony, during which he publicly acknowledges his guilt and pleads to a lesser charge. This last phase serves a variety of socially significant ends which have not been fully understood by commentators in the past. For example, George Herbert Mead indicates:

> Seemingly, without the criminal the cohesiveness of society would disappear, and the universal goods of the community would crumble into mutually repellent individual particles. The criminal does not seriously endanger the structure of society by his destructive activities . . . on the other hand he is responsible for a sense of solidarity, aroused among those whose attention would be otherwise centered upon interests quite divergent from those of each other. Thus courts of criminal justice may be essential to the preservation of society . . .[12]

Harold Garfinkel sees the "cop-out" as a "successful degradation ceremony." It is successful in that ultimate social values are reasserted. The accused is successfully stripped of a former status and recast in a manner acceptable to all the participants—perhaps even to himself.[13]

But these interpretations of the "cop-out" ceremony do not tell us the whole story. They fail to recognize the "cop-out" as an essential aspect of the panopticon effect. The "solidarity," "stripping," and "status degradation" are but superficialities of an altogether more vital and significant process. The "cop-out" ceremony is invaluable as a formally structured ritual for the benefit of significant *organizational* "others." The accused not only is made to assert publicly his guilt of a specific crime but to recite completely its details. He must further indicate that he is entering his plea of guilty freely, willingly, and voluntarily; and that he is not doing so because of any promises or in consideration of any commitments which anyone may have made to him. This last is intended as a blanket statement to shield the participants from any possible charges of coercion or undue influence in violation of due process requirements. Its function is to preclude any later review by an appellate court on these grounds and similarly to obviate any second thoughts an accused may develop about his plea.

The "cop-out" is in fact a charade, during which an accused must project an appropriate and acceptable degree of guilt, penitence, and remorse. If he adequately feigns the role of the "guilty person," his hearers will engage in the fantasy that he is contrite and thereby merits a lesser plea. One of the essential functions of the criminal lawyer is that he coach his accused-client in this performance. What is actually involved, therefore, is not a "degradation" or "reinforcing" process at all, but rather a highly structured system of exchange cloaked in the rituals of legalism and public professions of guilt and repentance. Everyone present is aware of the staging, including the defendant.

For the accused, his conception of self as a guilty person is largely temporary. In private he will quickly reassert his innocence. Almost immediately after his plea, and before sentencing, a defendant will be interviewed by a representative of the probation division in Metropolitan Court. The very first question asked by the probation officer is, "Are you guilty of the crime to which you pleaded?" This is by way of double affirmation of the defendant's guilt. Should the defendant now begin to make bold assertions of his innocence (these occur quite frequently despite pleas of guilt), he will be asked to withdraw his plea and stand trial on the original charges. The threat is in most cases sufficient to cause an accused to let the plea stand and to ask the probation officer to overlook his exclamations of innocence.

Table 5 shows the responses of a random sample of male defendants in Metropolitan Court during 1962, 1963, and 1964, in connection with their statements during pre-sentence probation interviews following their pleas of guilty:

Table 5: Defendant responses as to guilt or innocence after pleading
(1962–1963–1964)

Nature of response		Number of defendants	Per cent
Innocent (Manipulated)	"The lawyer or judge, police or DA 'conned me' "	86	11.9
Innocent (Pragmatic)	"Wanted to get it over with" "You can't beat the system" "They have you over a barrel when you have a record"	147	20.3
Innocent (Advice of counsel)	"Followed my lawyer's advice"	92	12.7
Innocent (Defiant)	"Framed"— Betrayed by "complainant," "police," "squealers," "lawyer," "friends," "wife," "girl friend"	33	4.6
Innocent (Adverse social data)	Blames probation officer or psychiatrist for "bad report" in cases where there was pre-pleading investigation	15	2.1
Guilty	"But I should have gotten a better deal" Blames lawyer, DA, police, judge	74	10.2
Guilty	Won't say anything further	21	2.9
Fatalistic (Doesn't press his "innocence," won't admit "guilt")	"I did it for convenience" "My lawyer told me it was the only thing I could do" "I did it because it was the best way out"	248	34.2
No response		8	1.1
TOTAL		724	100.0

As the data indicate, only a relatively small number (13.1 per cent) of defendants even admitted their guilt after the "cop-out" ceremony. Others, although they affirmed their guilt, felt they should have been able to negotiate a more favorable plea. The largest group of defendants (51.6 per cent) were those who reasserted their "innocence" after a public plea of guilty. These defendants showed different degrees of fervor, solemnity, and credibility, ranging from mild assertions of innocence, embroidered with a variety of stock explanations and rationalizations, to adamant claims of "framed." Thus the "innocents," for the most part, were largely concerned with underscoring for their probation interviewer their essential "goodness" and "worthiness," despite their formal plea of guilty. This assertion of innocence at the post-plea stage resurrects a more respectable and acceptable concept of self for the accused who has pleaded guilty. Many defendants mistakenly feel this will stand them in good stead at the time of sentence, or ultimately with probation or parole authorities.

Relatively few defendants (4.6 per cent) maintained they had been framed, but more (11.9 per cent) indicated they had been manipulated or "conned" by an agent-mediator to plead guilty.

A rather substantial group (20.3 per cent) preferred to stress the pragmatic aspects of their plea of guilty. They would only perfunctorily assert their innocence and would in general refer to some aspects of their situation which they believed hurt their bargaining leverage, including in some instances a prior criminal record.

The largest single group of defendants (34.2 per cent) were basically fatalistic. They could only offer weak suggestions of their innocence in rather halting terms and wholly without conviction. By the same token, they would not admit guilt readily and were generally evasive about guilt or innocence, preferring to stress their stoic submission. This sizable group of defendants appeared to see the court process as part of a monstrous organizational apparatus in which the defendant's role was not clearly defined. Reluctant to offend anyone in authority, fearful that clear-cut statements about their guilt or innocence might be wrongly interpreted, they adopted a stance of passivity, resignation, and acceptance. Interestingly, most named their lawyer as the one who crystallized the available alternatives for them, and who was therefore the critical element in their decision-making process.

In order to determine which agent-mediator was most influential in the accused's decision to plead or go to trial (regardless of the proposed basis of the plea), all of these defendants were asked to indicate the person who first suggested to them that they plead guilty. They were also asked to indicate which of the persons or officials who made such a suggestion was most influential in affecting their final decision to plead.

Table 6 shows the responses to the two questions:

Table 6: Role of agent-mediators in defendant's guilty plea

Person or official	First suggested plea of guilty		Influenced the accused most in his final decision to plead	
Judge	4	(.6%)	26	(3.6%)
District Attorney	67	(9.3%)	116	(16.0%)
Defense Counsel	407	(56.2%)	411	(56.7%)
Probation Officer	14	(1.9%)	3	(.4%)
Psychiatrist	8	(1.1%)	1	(.1%)
Relative (Wife)	34	(4.7%)	120	(16.6%)
Friends and Other relatives	21	(2.9%)	14	(1.9%)
Police	14	(1.9%)	4	(.6%)
Fellow inmates	119	(16.4%)	14	(1.9%)
Others	28	(3.9%)	5	(.7%)
"No response"	8	(1.1%)	10	(1.4%)
TOTAL	724	100.0%	724	99.9% *

* Rounded to nearest tenth.

It is popularly assumed that the police, through forced confessions, and the district attorney, with still other pressures, are most instrumental in convincing an accused to plead guilty. As Table 6 indicates, it is actually the *defendant's own counsel* who is most effective in this role. This phenomenon reinforces the extremely rational nature of criminal law administration, for an organization could not rely upon the sort of idiosyncratic measures employed by the police to induce confessions and maintain its efficiency, high production, and overall rational-legal character. The defense counsel becomes the ideal agent-mediator. As "officer of the court" and confidant of the accused and his kin group, he lives astride both worlds and can serve their ends as well as his own.

Because the defense counsel is such a crucial figure in the total organizational scheme, the same sample of defendants was asked to indicate at which stage of their contact with counsel was the suggestion of plea made. Table 7 shows the response for the kinds of defense counsel available in Metropolitan Court—legal aid, privately retained counsel, and counsel assigned by the court (but who may eventually be privately retained by the accused).

Table 7: Stage at which counsel suggested that accused plead

Stage of contact	Counsel Type					
	Privately retained		Legal aid		Assigned	
First	66	(34.7%)	237	(48.6%)	28	(59.6%)
Second	83	(43.7%)	142	(29.1%)	8	(17.0%)
Third	29	(15.3%)	63	(12.9%)	4	(8.5%)
Fourth or more	12	(6.3%)	31	(6.4%)	5	(10.6%)
"No response"	0	(0.0%)	14	(2.9%)	2	(4.3%)
TOTAL	190	100.0%	487	99.9% *	47	100.0%

* Rounded to nearest tenth.

The overwhelming majority of accused persons, regardless of type of counsel, related a specific incident which indicated that counsel suggested a guilty plea during the first or second contact. Of all the agent-mediators, the lawyer is most effective in manipulating an accused's perspectives, not withstanding previous pressures from police, the district attorney, the judge, or any others. Legal aid and assigned counsel are apparently more likely to suggest a possible plea at once. Perhaps they are responding to pressures of time and, in the case of an assigned counsel, the strong possibility that there will be no fee forthcoming.

Table 7 is further evidence of the perfunctory, ministerial character of the system in Metropolitan Court and similar courts. There is little real effort to individualize, and the lawyer's role as agent-mediator is unique: he is in effect a double agent. Although as "officer of the court" he mediates between the court organization and the defendant, his roles with respect to each are rent by conflicts of interests. Too often these must be resolved in favor of the organization which provides him with the means for his professional existence. Consequently, in order to reduce the strains and conflicts imposed in what is ultimately an overdemanding role obligation for him, the lawyer engages in a lawyer-client "confidence game."

We shall examine in detail, in chapters that follow, the significant professional personnel of the criminal court. We shall attempt to identify not only the nature of their recruitment, career lines, and profesional ideologies, but also the manner in which the court organization alters their traditional professional roles. They respond to organizational demands and rules by abandoning their ideological and professional commitments.

5

The lawyer as agent-mediator

> "Have you a criminal lawyer in this burg?"
> "We think so, but we haven't been able to prove it on him."
> —Carl Sandburg, *The People, Yes*

Three landmark Supreme Court decisions dealing with the role of the lawyer have been hailed as destined to effect profound changes in the administration of criminal law in America. The first of these, *Gideon vs. Wainwright* (1963), requires states and localities to furnish counsel for indigent persons charged with a felony. The Gideon ruling raised an interesting question: what is the precise point in time at which a suspect is entitled to a lawyer? The answer came relatively quickly in *Escobedo vs. Illinois* (1964), which aroused a storm of controversy.

Danny Escobedo confessed to the murder of his brother-in-law after the police had refused to allow retained counsel to see him, although his lawyer was present in the station house and asked to confer with his client. In a 5 to 4 decision, the Supreme Court asserted that when the process of police investigation shifts from merely investigatory to accusatory—"when its focus is on the accused and its purpose is to elicit a confession—our adversary system begins to operate, and, under the circumstances here, the accused must be permitted to consult with his lawyer." Escobedo's confession was rendered inadmissible, triggering a national debate among police, district attorneys, judges, lawyers, and other law enforcement officials, which continues unabated, about the value and propriety of confessions in criminal cases.

Subsequently, on June 13, 1966, in another 5 to 4 decision, the court underscored the principle enunciated in *Escobedo* in the case of *Miranda vs. Arizona.* An accused must be advised of his right to remain silent and to have an attorney. Police interrogation of any suspect in custody, without his consent, unless a defense attorney is present, is prohibited by the self-incrimination provision of the Fifth Amendment.

In the *Gideon, Escobedo,* and *Miranda* cases, the Supreme Court reiterated the traditional legal concept of a defense lawyer. As counsel in an *adversary, combative* proceeding, he assiduously musters all the admittedly limited resources at his command to defend the accused. But does the Supreme Court's conception of the role of counsel in a criminal case square with social reality? Is the court's assumption warranted that in these cases defense counsel will conduct a combative, adversary defense of the accused?

The varied organizational contexts in which the defense counsel acts, and in which the dimensions of his role are structured, have not been considered by the court in these cases. Perhaps at the gatehouse level (police, prosecution) it would be a simple matter for any lawyer to advise a client to remain silent. But at the mansion level (criminal court) there is a very limited understanding of the real functions of defense counsel.

It is the lawyer who, in large measure, "ties together" the seemingly disparate elements of police, prosecution, and court organization to help them dispose of a voluminous case load. Although he performs a critical function in the legal system, the criminal lawyer is a marginal practitioner. He does the "dirty work" of the profession and is often shunned by his more respected and powerful colleagues. Yet his delicate agent-mediator role is not at all unique in the legal profession, in terms of the historical and organizational contexts in which lawyers have always functioned.

In the American colonies, lawyers as a group were the subject of widespread scorn and mistrust. The people felt that they profited from the misfortunes and misery of others. It was therefore not unusual for an individual to plead his own case, and in early Massachusetts it was in fact illegal for a lawyer to accept a fee. But with increased settlement and the expansion of trade and commerce, there was a striking increase in the number of transactions involving the need for legal expertise. Simultaneously, the bar developed as an important source of wealth and social prestige, and by the time of the American Revolution important members of the colonial elites were lawyers or those trained in law.[1] Of the fifty-six signers of the Declaration of Independence, twenty-five were lawyers. Thirty-one of the fifty-five men who served in the Continental Congress were lawyers. Three hundred and fifteen of the 535 members of the 88th Congress were lawyers.[2] Since 1900 lawyers have provided approximately one-fourth of all the state legislators in the nation, and to that extent they are overwhelmingly over-represented as an occupational group in the various state legislatures.[3] Most state governors are lawyers, as are many administrators in the executive and legislative branches of local and federal government, as well as the usual judicial offices.[4]

While de Tocqueville saw the proliferation of the legal profession into virtually every area of American life as a salutary development —because lawyers would act as a check upon the impetuosities and tyrannies of the masses—later commentators have deplored their role. Some modern spokesmen see the lawyer as an individual whose talents and skills are for sale to the highest bidder, serving the particular vested interest that has purchased his services for the moment. The higher claims of community and society are secondary. No less a figure than Chief Justice Harlan F. Stone once indicated that the members of the legal profession as a group had assumed the "morals of the marketplace." [5] In drama and in poetry, the lawyer has been excoriated and censured. At one point, Shakespeare has one of his characters exclaim,"The first thing we do, let's kill all the lawyers." [6] Carl Sandburg, talking about various forms of thievery and chicane, caustically avers, "A farmer between two lawyers is a fish between two cats." [7]

In an acrimonious barb, Thorstein Veblen asserted:

> The profession of the law does not imply large ownership; but since no taint of usefulness, for other than competitive purposes, attaches to the lawyer's trade, it grades high in the conventional scheme. The lawyer is exclusively occupied with the details of predatory fraud, either in achieving or checkmating chicane, and success in the profession is therefore accepted as marking a large endowment of that barbarian astuteness which has always commanded man's respect and fear.[8]

The image of the lawyer in literature as a crafty, scheming, deceitful individual is perhaps a reflection not only of continuing mistrust but of a vague feeling that lawyers are wholly dispensable. Nevertheless, the occupation continues to command high prestige. Between two studies by the National Opinion Research Center, one in 1947 and another in 1963, the lawyer actually gained in prestige rating—from high to higher.[9] The relatively high earnings of the legal profession show up in a life style that is desirable for imitation, so lawyers are awarded high occupational prestige regardless of other considerations. Although there are wide earning disparities between them, all appear to be subsumed under the rubric of "lawyer." [10] Their status is to some extent conditioned by the access lawyers have to wealth and the possessors of wealth.

The idea of training in law as a vehicle of upward social mobility appears to be exaggerated, but it is nevertheless widely accepted. Napoleon's exhortation to his troops that the lowest common soldier in the ranks carried a marshal's baton in his knapsack finds its counterpart in the legal profession. Since the time of the American Revolution legal training has been considered a useful adjunct to many careers outside the practice of law itself. The rigorous, methodical patterns of intellectual discipline in studying law are thought to be highly adaptive for other occupations. In many upper-class families, it has been traditional for at least one son to attend an Ivy League law school, if he were able to do so. In all classes, law is viewed as an excellent training ground for many activities in government service. According to Suzanne Keller: "Within the business elite of 1950, one-sixth were trained as lawyers; within the diplomatic elite for the century, two-fifths; and within the political elite, one half. (As to the Supreme Court justices, all, of course, were lawyers.)" [11]

The close nexus between law and politics has no counterpart in the experience of other Western nations. But, by virtue of their training, skills, and work opportunities, the lawyer's career in America is almost the natural concomitant of the political career. The two career cycles complement each other, and much of the lawyer's time is devoted to establishing the necessary "contacts" for business. A lawyer does not really leave his practice or business behind when he goes to Congress or the legislature; he has simply expanded his venture by opening a branch office, free of the expense usually involved.

The law is a career that continues to be fraught with possibilities, if not promise, for the upwardly mobile individual. Important statuses in American society are filled and recruited from the ranks of the legal profession. Much of the ambivalence toward lawyers in America is due to their interstitial role—although they are often simply carrying out the predatory designs of their clients.

THE ALLOCATION OF LEGAL SERVICES AND CAREERS

The allocation of legal services, their character and quality, their distribution among the publics being served, the recruitment and career lines of those performing these services, are in large measure a function of the stratification system.[12] The American Bar Foundation reports that in 1960 there were 285,933 lawyers engaged in some form of legal practice in the United States.[13] Of this total, some 192,351 were wholly engaged in private practice, not connected with employment in any public or semi-public agency. The same organization reported that in 1958, 52 per cent of the lawyers in the nation were engaged in individual, private practice, 28 per cent were lawyers in firms, and 20 per cent were engaged in various kinds of practice other than private, such as house counsel for a corporation, a government legal department, or other public employment for a salary.[14] While there may be some duplication in the total figures, most authorities agree on the total number of lawyers and their distribution in practice.

Income statistics are somewhat confusing and can be misleading, because so many variables are involved. It is of course crucial whether one is a partner or merely an associate in a firm; whether one is engaged in solo private practice or is employed in a public agency (and whether the agency is federal, state, or municipal); whether one is engaged in trial work, appellate work, or drafting of statutes and legal documents. Other important variables are the kind of practice—for example, corporate, matrimonial (divorce cases), criminal work, or negligence—and, finally, the stage of one's legal career.

In private practice, income will be closely related to the size of the firm. Generally speaking, the larger the firm, the greater the melon to be sliced. One study indicates that lawyers practicing in the upper levels of the profession (for example, corporate work) will have an income 70 per cent higher than those practicing at the lower level (such as negligence or collection work). Upper-level lawyers reported a median annual income of $14,500 as compared with $8,500 at the lower level.[15] Of course, operating expenses for various types of practices will differ, and statements of gross earnings are quite meaningless unless this factor is taken into consideration. The law is a business and must be viewed as such regardless of any professional character it may possess; and one writer has indicated that the operating expenses of a large Wall Street factory-type firm can amount to about half its gross revenue.[16] In addition, the nature of law practice affords the opportunity to conceal income, so that published figures of lawyer income are at best problematic. It can be stated as a matter of general accuracy, however, that the most lucrative practices, where salaries for partners may range from $50,000 to $250,000 per year (and operating expenses almost $3 million per year), are those large urban firms whose specialties are corporate reorganization, anti-trust work, trust indentures, and the like. Here, "law practice" becomes highly bureaucratic in terms of the division of labor, although recruiting by the large firm remains highly particularistic and discriminates against graduates of other than national law schools, women, Jews, and other ethnics.[17] Beneath the top level, lawyer income drops according to size of firm, with the lowest income and the least desirable type of practice (negligence, criminal work, collection work) being found at the level of the single, private practitioner who may earn as little as $5,000 per year.

Like the practice of medicine, the legal profession has downgraded the "general practitioner," leaving him behind in terms of rewards and opportunities. The old-fashioned "family lawyer" has been fragmented into a proliferation of specialties, which have intensified certain caste-like qualities in the profession. The lawyer as a folk hero, a Clarence Darrow waging a never-ending battle to right wrongs in the service of aggrieved persons and the downtrodden, is no more. In contrast to de Tocqueville and Bryce, Harold Laski could say:

> The character of the profession has changed because the greatest rewards it can offer now come not to the lawyer who is an eminent advocate, not to the general practitioner who looks after the little client, in the little case . . . but to the lawyer who devotes himself to advising the vast corporations and combines which now dominate American economic life. . . . Lawyers have been the guardians of immense vested interests. . . . They have,

indeed, built a partnership between themselves and Big Business which has often seemed a barrier to all social change. They are rarely interested in the law, and still more rarely in its relation to justice.[18]

The growing ties of lawyers to corporate and business enterprises has been noted by the American Bar Association itself, which has indicated that "there is a class relationship between the incomes of lawyers, by states, and the incomes after taxes of the corporations of the corresponding states . . . the number of lawyers who are serving a single corporation's interests is steadily growing." Lawyers have become very much part of the organizations they serve—as board members, legal technicians, and often in capacities not even remotely related to the practice of law. They are involved and enmeshed in decisions involving advertising policy, trade and price wars, union negotiations, lobbying, financing, procurement of government contracts, and activities more appropriately those of a business administrator or salesman. Their institutional loyalties are closely tied to and formulated by the economic interests and requirements of their organization. For increasingly, whether they serve in the corporation, the large law firm, or in similar institutional settings, they are deprofessionalized.

Even in civil cases, most lawyers rarely see the inside of a court any more, for litigation is not only costly and time consuming but also risky. The general litigation that does occur is frequently at the lower levels of law practice—non-support and matrimonial suits, minor surrogate and realty matters, collection suits, landlord-tenant cases, some criminal trials, negligence actions, and judicial reviews of administrative decisions. Usually these are not as lucrative as a corporate matter involving unfair competition, patent infringement, stockholders' suits, or a corporate reorganization, which may command fees in the millions.

Thus the best-trained, most highly skilled, and most actively recruited lawyers are drawn to the corporate, large-scale, bureaucratic type of practice which offers the highest rewards. Those in private practice, either individual or in small firms (who constitute the majority of lawyers), perform the overwhelming number of small but socially important tasks, working with lower- and middle-class clients. The poorest of these must resort to legal aid services, whose quality and availability vary greatly across the nation.

Published studies conclude that the minority group member, the ethnic, the individual educated in a part-time law school, the son of a laboring father, and the Jew or Catholic are likely to be engaged in individual practice and "end up doing the 'dirty work' of the bar: personal injury, divorce, criminal work, collections, title searching, etc." [19] Further, since approximately 90 per cent of those who appear in a criminal court are persons in the lower class, their limited resources will furnish them with the least-qualified lawyers for their defense.

THE LAWYERS OF METROPOLITAN COURT

Before the Gideon case there were four types of legal assistance for indigent accused persons: assignment of a lawyer by the court as each case arose; privately financed legal aid defenders; public defenders supported by public funds; and mixed public and private legal aid systems. But there has been widespread dissatisfaction with these services and general criticism of the organized bar in meeting its obligations toward accused persons. Chief Justice Earl Warren has been critical of the legal profession, indicating that "it did not reflect credit on the legal profession when prisoners with meritorious defenses had to write petitions to the Supreme Court in their own hand—writing from their cells." [20] It is also generally agreed that public defender systems, where they exist, are not sufficiently independent of the prosecution, that "the accusatorial system comes close to being an inquisitorial system."

Although the Metropolitan Court legal aid system receives both public and private funds, it conceives of itself as "entirely independent" of the court structure in which it functions. It helps to dispose of approximately 70 per cent of the Metropolitan Court case load each year but unrealistically sees itself as not "involved" in the affairs, designs, and goals of the court organization. The legal aid office prefers to maintain an adversary pose. The overall impression of court personnel, lawyers, and legal aid people is that indigent accused persons represented by legal aid in certain crime categories will fare at least as well as privately represented defendants. Indeed, many attorneys and probation officers think the legal aid staff does better for its client in certain instances than the non-political attorney who is not a Metropolitan Court "regular."

Of the remaining 30 per cent of cases not handled by legal aid, approximately one-third are the source of practice of seventeen attorneys who are "court regulars" in Metropolitan Court. Unlike the criminal lawyer we have described elsewhere, at least twelve of these lawyers are persons of great intellectual and professional skills and political sophistication. The criminal bar of Metropolitan Court are not nondescript, professionally disgruntled, inadequately trained plebians. In dress, speech, manner, erudition, and legal sophistication, they are more than a match for the Wall Street lawyer. In fact, they are often called upon by "downtown firms" to represent an upper-class client who has been indicted. While the "downtown" large firm lawyer eschews criminal work and abhors those in it, he is usually terribly insecure in a courtroom— especially in a court like Metropolitan Court. The seventeen lawyers who appear in most of the trials in Metropolitan Court are reputed to possess the necessary skills for such activity. If so, their elaborate skills are under-utilized, because their capacities for negotiation and the charismatic quality of their reputations are the real mainstays of their professional activity. And because they are so intricately enmeshed in the court organization, they cease being true professionals and instead function as "fixers" for a fee.

Bargaining for a plea takes place at three different levels—with the district attorney, the judge, and even with probation officials, if that organization has been asked to make a pre-pleading investigation. Ordinarily the prosecution has a crude index to the "worth" of a case, based on how "healthy" it is (i.e., whether the charges can be proved beyond a reasonable doubt), harm to the complainant, possibilities of restitution, and the yellow sheet (rap sheet or prior record) of the accused. But the overriding dimension is seldom discussed: what offenses are currently more opprobious than others and merit special attention. These are "worth" much more in terms of the plea to be taken or permitted. Thus, for example, at times drug offenses will be treated quite lightly and be "worth" very little, and the prosecution will allow lesser pleas to minor offenses to cover a felony offense for sale or possession of drugs. But should there be a public furor over drugs, then drug cases appreciate greatly. Regardless of the variables involved, the plea that is generally accepted is one that will afford an "adequate scope of punishment"; this is the main consideration in Metropolitan Court and elsewhere.

The lawyer-regular has an ongoing "account" with the prosecution office which he can draw upon from time to time to meet the exigencies of a particular case. The legal-aid group, too, can often negotiate a quite reasonable plea for an indigent defendant because of its close relationship with the prosecutor's office—if the accused impresses his free lawyer, as well as the prosecution, with his "worthiness." Judges are ordinarily not supposed to be involved in this bargaining process, nor are they to make any commitments about the sentence to be imposed in return for a specific plea. Despite these proscriptions, lawyer regulars in Metropolitan Court are always in three-way communication with the assistant district attorney and the judge's chambers, in order to smooth out any differences over a specific plea. Visits to the judge's chambers to establish the sentence in advance are routine. Beyond the technique of "calendaring" a case so that it appears before a "favorable" judge, lawyer regulars, through their clubhouse ties with the members of the bench, are able to augment the value of their stock in trade through the political "account" they have with some judges. So there is a continuous procession of lawyer regulars between prosecution office and judge's chambers to establish plea and sentence before the anticlimactic public "cop-out" ceremony.

Because so much of their activity is "fixing," Metropolitan Court regulars appraise themselves rather critically. All of them indicate that they rarely have a genuine opportunity to exercise their "real professional skills." They blame "the system." They are quick to admit that they feel inadequate in dealing with the court as an organization and that they "play the game" in order to "get along." They perceive dimly that their independence is a myth and that their continued role in the court, and its accompanying comfortable income, are wholly dependent upon favorable organizational relations. Although their income is relatively good vis-à-vis other lawyers, Metropolitan Court regulars see themselves engaged in a law practice which is less than honorable.

But they point an accusing finger at the "fat cats" in the "downtown firms" who, they claim, perform services of lesser social importance, charge "exorbitant" fees, and nevertheless are assigned high prestige. Thus, despite their advantages, Metropolitan Court lawyers see themselves as marginal, peripheral individuals. In short, they accept the legal profession's definition of their status and prestige. Most of the lawyers in Metropolitan Court say they would enter other professions than the law "if I could do it over again." These same individuals would not want their children to be lawyers—or at least not to practice criminal law. "You're everyone's goat"—"a patsy," "no matter how a case comes out—you lose in the eyes of your client." "You're caught in the middle— even when you've won a tough trial, the client complains. You've reduced a felonious assault to a disorderly conduct charge—still they're not satisfied. Favors anyone else owes you are mere trivialities, something easily forgotten. But favors I owe a cop, a bondsman, a DA, a judge, or another lawyer become irrevocable obligations. Apart from the money, the only real satisfaction in this business is that at least you're really doing something for the client as well as society."

Not all Metropolitan Court lawyers think their career is without importance. Some of the regulars insist that criminal law is one of the few areas of the law where genuine professional, independent practice is possible. One of them, an Ivy League law school graduate, spoke of an earlier aspect of his professional development in a somewhat traumatic vein:

"After law school, I landed a job with one of the largest law firms in the country, the kind that has fifteen partners and employs nearly one hundred lawyers. Some of the original partners were dead, but their names were kept on the firm stationery anyway—to maintain tradition and clients. They occupied five stories in a downtown office skyscraper, and really, the best way to describe the physical setup would be to say that it looked like a 'mahogany forest,' or perhaps I should say 'jungle.' In any event, I spent ten years there before I found out I was nothing more than a grown-up errand boy with a law degree, or at best some partner's faceless memorandum writer.

"Each partner had at his disposal a group of 'associates' who did all of his researching, drafting, brief writing, and the usual legwork on various matters. Often you would never know the nature of the matter or the dimensions of the problem you were working on. An assignment would ordinarily begin with being summoned to a partner's office, rarely with a memorandum requesting service. The way we were summoned is worth mentioning. There was a system of bells. Each associate had a prescribed number of bells which signaled that he was wanted in the partner's office. Four bells meant me. So you would get your marching orders, and when there was some measure of urgency—and there usually was—you would find yourself working twelve to fourteen hours a day, including weekends. At first I didn't mind what was, in retrospect, a crude system of exploitation. I was getting what I considered valuable experience in my profession, and besides, there were salary increases—and always the tacit possibility of advancing to a junior partnership. As the years wore on, I knew that although I was useful I was never to be more than a salaried employee, like any other white-collar slave. My disgust with the pretended professionalism and the phony low-pressure amenities of the place began to show, especially after two incidents of advancement based on nepotism occurred in the firm.

"In time I became openly critical of the firm's policies and practices, increasingly dissatisfied with myself and with the kind of law practice where you are simply a puppet for some partner who pulls all the strings and calls all the plays. I then began to get some not too subtle hints about my 'attitude' and was admonished for not being a 'team' person.

"It came time to part. But you don't really get fired. You get sacked in stages. Slowly, the matters and jobs referred to you diminish to a trickle. Finally, you have no work on your agenda at all, and you will sit there twiddling your thumbs. But long before that, even someone who is dense will take the hint. I have often since imagined that if you didn't take the hint and resign, then slowly the appurtenances of your office would begin to disappear—stripped bare, piece by piece, until only the telephone was standing on the bare floor. So I quit and entered private practice, and here I am. At least I'm my own boss."

The Metropolitan Court regular makes no effort to conceal his close, intimate relations with all levels of court personnel. These informal relations are the *sine qua non* not only for maintaining and building his practice but for the negotiation of pleas and sentences. The individuals to whom he "owes favors" include police and bondsmen who have steered business his way, or court clerks and probation personnel who have kept him abreast of developments in a given case so that he can appear to have "secret" knowledge for the benefit of his client and the accused's kin group. The practice of law is largely a matter of personal influence.

While the legal aid defender is likely to have many of the civil-service career characteristics of his counterpart in the office of the district attorney, the seventeen court regulars and the other lawyers in Metropolitan Court see themselves as "independent" businessmen. The mean age of the regulars is fifty-four years, somewhat older than the judges. Two of the seventeen are women.

All have been active politically, some for over thirty years, some having missed an appointment to the bench by a political quirk or upset. Seven are graduates of "national" law schools, and two of these are graduates of Ivy League schools. Of the remaining ten regulars, all but four have had law training at a university-connected school. Seven of the seventeen were affiliated with the district attorney's office before going into private practice. Almost all have had a career background in criminal law while doing occasional negligence, matrimonial, and estate work. The comment of one of them fairly sums up the attitude of the rest in this regard: "I got out of law school and found law practice to be positively dull, a total bore. My first real opportunity that offered me any sense of involvement was criminal law. I made my life here. Everyone I know, all my contacts are here. Even though we can't really do too much for our clients, we're doing important work. I'm on my own and making a damn good living at it."

These lawyers are second- and third-generation Americans, seven of whom are the children of lower middle-class, non-manual workers; two are from lower-class families. Eight are the children of professional fathers and medium-sized mercantile families. Nine are Jewish, including the two women; seven are Catholics; the only Protestant is the only Negro regular. There have been more Negroes and various Spanish-speaking ethnics among non-regular lawyers in recent years; while they may recruit clients on the basis of racial and ethnic "contacts," they often turn an important case over to a court regular under a private arrangement.

The regulars' earnings are well above the national average for lawyers. While figures of this kind are often suspect, corroborative evidence indicates a mean annual income of $18,000. This is net, after payments for "favors," "gifts," and other costs of "doing business" in the criminal court have been deducted. There is no way of establishing what these expenses can amount to in actual payments. One lawyer admitted spending as much as $2,500 to $3,000 a year in that manner, to nurture "good will" toward him and his practice.

THE PRACTICE OF LAW AS A CONFIDENCE GAME

The real key to understanding the role of defense counsel in a criminal case is the fixing and collection of his fee. It is a problem which influences to a significant degree the criminal court process itself, not just the relationship of the lawyer and his client. In essence, a lawyer-client "confidence game" is played.

In many "server-served" relationships for a fee—which include not only the practice of law, medicine, or dentistry but also plumbing—there is not always a visible end-product or tangible service involved. A plumber, for example, will usually be able to show that he has performed a service by unstopping a drain, repairing a leaky faucet or pipe—and therefore merits his fee. He has rendered a tangible benefit for his client in return for the requested fee. On the other hand, a physician who has not performed some visible surgery or otherwise discernible procedure may be accused by the patient of having "done nothing" for him. Doctors may even prescribe or administer by injection a placebo to overcome a patient's potential dissatisfaction in paying a fee "for nothing."

The lawyer has a special problem in this regard, no matter what his status or prestige. Much legal work is intangible, because it is simply a few words of advice, some preventive action, a telephone call, negotiation of some kind, a form filled out and filed, a hurried conference with another attorney or an official of a government agency, a letter or opinion written, or a countless variety of seemingly innocuous and even prosaic procedures and actions. These are the basic activities of almost all lawyers at all levels of practice. They represent not precise professional skills but rather the acts of a broker, agent, sales representative, or lobbyist. The lawyer pursues someone else's interests and designs.

The large-scale law firm may not speak as openly of its "contacts" and "fixing" abilities as does the lower-level lawyer. It trades instead upon the façade of thick carpeting, walnut paneling, genteel low pressure, and superficialities of traditional legal professionalism. But even the large firm may be challenged because the services rendered or results obtained do not appear to merit the fee asked. Thus there is a recurrent problem in the legal profession in fixing the fee and justifying it.

In a criminal case, the defendant is soon parted from the spoils he may have acquired from his illicit activities. Not infrequently, the returns from his larceny are sequestered by a defense lawyer in payment of fee. Inevitably, the amount of the fee is close to the dollar value of the crime committed. On occasion, defendants have been known to commit additional offenses while at liberty on bail, in order to get money for payment of legal fees. Defense lawyers make sure that even the most obtuse clients know there is a firm connection between fee payment and the zealous exercise of professional expertise, secret knowledge, and organizational "connections" in their behalf. They try to keep their clients at the precise edge of anxiety calculated to encourage prompt payment of fee. The client's attitude in this relationship is often a precarious admixture of hostility, mistrust, dependence, and sycophancy. By playing upon his client's anxieties and establishing a seemingly causal relationship between the fee and the accused's extrication from his difficulties, the lawyer establishes the necessary groundwork to assure a minimum of haggling over the fee and its eventual payment.

The lawyer must then be sure to manipulate the client and stage manage the case so that help and service at least *appear* to be rendered. This is accomplished in several ways. At the outset, the lawyer uses a measure of sales puff which may range from unbounding self-confidence to complete arrogance. This will be supplemented by a studied, faultless mode of personal attire. In the larger firms, the furnishings and office trappings will serve as the backdrop for impressing and intimidating the client. In all firms, solo or large scale, an access to secret knowledge and to the seats of power and influence is implied as the basic vendible commodity.

The special complication of the criminal lawyer is that an accused always "loses," even when he has been exonerated by an acquittal, discharge, or dismissal. His hostility is directed, by means of displacement, toward his lawyer, and in this sense a criminal lawyer never really "wins" a case. The really satisfied client is rare, because even an accused's vindication leaves him with some degree of dissatisfaction and hostility. The man who is sentenced to jail may of course be a singularly unappreciative client.

Bearing these attitudes in mind, the criminal lawyer collects his fee *in advance*. Often, because the lawyer and the accused both have questionable designs upon each other, the lawyer plays the confidence game. First, he must arrange for his fee; second, he must prepare his client for defeat (a highly likely contingency) and then, if necessary, "cool him out"; third, he must satisfy the court organization that he has adequately negotiated the plea so as to preclude an embarrassing incident which might invite "outside" scrutiny.

If the accused is himself unable to pay more than a token fee, the lawyer must involve as many of the accused's kin group as possible in the situation. This is especially so if he hopes to collect a significant part of a proposed substantial fee. It is not uncommon for several relatives to contribute toward the fee. The larger the group, the greater the possibility that the lawyer will collect a sizable fee by exacting several contributions.

A fee for a felony case which ultimately results in a plea, rather than a trial, may ordinarily range anywhere from $500 to $1,500. Should the case go to trial, the fee will be proportionately larger, depending upon the length of the trial. But the larger the fee the lawyer wishes to exact, the more impressive his performance must be; he must show himself to be of great influence and power in the court organization. To some extent court personnel will aid the lawyer in creating and maintaining an image. This is the partial basis for the quid pro quo that exists between the lawyer and the court organization. It is the continuing basis for the lawyer's higher loyalty to the organization; his relationship with his client, in contrast, is transient, ephemeral, and often superficial.

The lawyer has often been accused of stirring up unnecessary litigation, especially in the field of negligence. He is said to acquire a vested interest in an action or claim which would otherwise never have developed. The criminal lawyer develops a vested interest of a different nature: not to promote the litigation but to limit its scope and duration. Only in this way can a case be "profitable." Thus he enlists the aid of relatives not only to assure payment of his fee but to help him in his agent-mediator role of convincing the accused to plead guilty, and ultimately to help him in "cooling out" the accused, if necessary.[21]

The fee is often collected in stages, each installment payable before a necessary court appearance during an accused's career journey. At each stage, in his interviews and communications with the accused (and with members of his kin group, if they are helping with the fee payment), the lawyer employs an air of professional confidence and "inside-dopesterism" to assuage anxieties on all sides. He makes the necessary bland assurances and in effect manipulates his client, who is usually willing to do and say the things—true or not—that will help his attorney extricate him. Because what he is selling is not measurable, the lawyer can make extravagant claims of influence and secret knowledge with impunity. But, as in a genuine confidence game, the victim who has participated is loath to do anything that will upset the lesser plea which his lawyer has "conned" him into accepting.

In his role as double agent, the criminal lawyer performs an extremely vital and delicate mission for the court organization and the accused. Both principals are anxious to terminate the litigation with a minimum of expense and damage. No one else in the court structure is more strategically located, more ideally suited to do so than the lawyer. In recognition of this, judges will cooperate with attorneys in many important ways. For example, they will recess the case of an accused who is in jail awaiting plea or sentence if the attorney requests such action. Overtly this may be done for some innocuous and seemingly valid reason, but the real purpose is to permit the attorney to press for the collection of his fee, which he knows he will probably not get if the case is concluded. Judges are aware of this tactic, but they will go along with it on the grounds that important ends are being served.

The judge may also lend the official aura of his office and courtroom so that a lawyer can stage manage an "all-out" performance for the accused in justification of his fee. The judge and other court personnel will serve as backdrop for a scene charged with dramatic fire, in which the accused's lawyer makes a stirring appeal in his behalf. With a show of restrained passion, the lawyer will intone the virtues of the accused and recite the social deprivations that have reduced him to his present state. The speech varies somewhat, depending on whether the accused has been convicted after trial or has pleaded guilty. In the main, however, the incongruity, superficiality, and ritualistic character of the total performance is understood by a visibly impassive, almost bored reaction on the part of the judge and other members of the court retinue. Afterward, there is a hearty exchange of pleasantries between the lawyer and district attorney, wholly out of context with the supposed adversary nature of the preceding events. The fiery passion is gone, and lawyers for both sides resume their offstage relations, chatting amiably and perhaps including the judge in their restrained banter. No other aspect of their visible conduct so effectively puts even a casual observer on notice that these individuals have claims upon each other. In intricacy and depth, their relations range far beyond the priorities or claims of a particular defendant.

Criminal law is a unique form of private law practice. It simply *appears* to be private practice. Actually, it is bureaucratic practice, because of the lawyer's role in the authority, discipline, and perspectives of the court organization. Private practice, in a professional sense, supposedly involves the maintenance of an organized, disciplined body of knowledge and learning; the lawyer is imbued with a spirit of autonomy and service, the earning of a livelihood being incidental. But the lawyer in the criminal court is a double agent, serving higher organizational rather than professional ends. The lawyer-client "confidence game," in addition to its other functions, helps to conceal this fact.

6

The judge as bureaucrat

> "I must say that, as a litigant, I should dread a lawsuit beyond almost anything else short of sickness and death."
>
> —Judge Learned Hand

Of the 8,180 judges officially reported in the courts of America, 599 are on the federal bench, 5,301 are state or county judges, and 2,280 sit in city courts.[1] Many other thousands serve in police courts or as justices of the peace, although many of these have other occupations. Perhaps as many as 5 per cent of the country's approximately 285,000 lawyers are thus serving as judges at any one time.

The judiciary is one of the few occupations which enjoys extremely high status in practically all industrial urban cultures.[2] Its enormous prestige in America can be seen in situations involving judges which have provoked public attention. The discussion over the mysterious disappearance in 1930 of New York's Judge Crater continues to this day because it is inconceivable that a judge would disappear voluntarily. When federal Judge Manton was found guilty in 1939 of accepting bribes, the expectations of his high office were so stridently violated that the case occasioned much comment. In similar fashion, the convictions in 1964 of Judges Melvin L. Osterman and J. Vincent Keogh of New York on charges of bribery aroused a furor in the news media and raised many questions about the nature of our whole judicial system.[3] Judges are assumed to be immune from such temptation, in contrast to more ordinary mortals.

Judicial biographies have generally emphasized judgeship in the "grand" tradition.[4] They are for the most part paeans of praise and adulatory studies, revealing little of the judge's actual work role. In the main they concern themselves with judges who have established careers in the higher appellate courts, far removed from the administrative fray of the lower civil and criminal courts. But much of the charismatic quality of the judge flows from the "grand" tradition and its accompanying mystique. There seems to be little that is intellectually exciting or grandiose in the career of a judge at the lowest level. He is so close to the publics served daily by the bench and bar that, while he may retain the charismatic flavor of the office, his reputation becomes tarnished and somewhat mundane. He bears the brunt of criticism and dissatisfaction with the legal system, and especially with the administration of the criminal law. In the prestige hierarchy of judges and lawyers, those in the criminal courts are in the lower levels, however important their work is. The civil courts, which oversee the orderly transfer of wealth in our society by their appointment of receivers, executors, administrators, trustees, guardians, and other caretakers of property, are considered far more important areas of practice—and sources of remuneration. This "prestige gap" is an important source of the profound feelings of marginality that plague judges and lawyers alike in the criminal court.

Few of the judges serving in the trial courts have been memorialized, so we know little of real value about the real "infantrymen" of the entire legal system. For it is they who ultimately stage manage and direct the drama that occurs in the lower courts. With the defense lawyer in the criminal court, they make the system of criminal justice work. Without the judge's active involvement, in pursuit of rational values in disposing of the maximum number of pleas, the entire system of criminal justice would founder.

Despite the fact that the upper-level judge serves as the role model in literature, there are at least three levels of the judicial career line. The Lower Level is available and followed by most lawyers who become judges. Quite simply, this level has the most positions to offer, and they are manipulated as patronage plums at the clubhouse level of local politics. The judicial career aspirant at this level has usually attended a proprietary or part-time law school of dubious quality, whose major emphasis is on preparing its graduates for the state bar examination. A marginal member of his profession, he may trade upon his ethnicity and translate his rather strong personal mobility aspirations into a cluster of contacts in his local political club, as well as a variety of memberships in fraternal, benevolent, and religious organizations. A lawyer at this stage of his career can look forward to a long apprenticeship—possibly most of his adult life—performing a wide range of legal and other services in return for the occasional legal business which may bring a meaningful fee. The number of judicial candidates far exceeds the available posts, so most aspirants are doomed to disappointment. Clubhouse lawyer regulars often find that they have dedicated most of a lifetime of law practice to the club, only to find judicial or other rewards snatched from them by nepotism or other higher claims.

The law practice of the upwardly mobile clubhouse ethnic often reflects the status limitations and concerns of his clients. "Italian," "Irish," "Puerto Rican," and "Jewish" lawyers find that their client appeal is not based on their intrinsic skills but rather on their presumed ethnic characteristics. Lawyers learn early in their career to exploit ethnic loyalties in securing practice as well

as in their political life. Their law practice at this level is largely
of the negligence, landlord-tenant, criminal work variety, and most
court appearances, if any, occur in the lower-level courts where
their clubhouse brethren sit as judges. Thus the clubhouse becomes an important career nexus not only for the judicial or political aspirant but as a source of "contacts" so necessary to a busy
law practice.

Wallace Sayre and Herbert Kaufman indicated recently that the
"going rate" for judgeships in New York City was the equivalent
of two years' salary contributed to the political party.[5] Although
most Metropolitan Court judges have a lower-level career line,
their incumbency has been free of the usual taint of rumors so
prevalent elsewhere about paying for a seat on the bench. Nevertheless, their ascendancy to the bench was preceded by many
years of clubhouse activity, including heavy contributions of time
and money to party activities. These contributions continue, because strong clubhouse ties are needed for re-election or promotion. The situation generates commitments and obligations to "politically visible" lawyers in Metropolitan Court, who in turn feel
entitled to some sort of quid pro quo for their long years of service to the club. If they cannot receive payment in cash, they will
accept payment "in kind"—judicial favors dispensed at critical
junctures in the criminal lawyer's practice.

The lower-level judicial career, then, has a built-in socialization
process. It assures the early acceptance of clubhouse norms and
expectancies with regard to the character of future conduct on the
bench, should one be designated to run for the office. Those who
are not picked will often seek posts as law assistants and law
secretaries, which they regard as a favorable career compromise.
These positions are considered critical in the power structure, because they conduct a good deal of the "judge's business" at the
lower level and act as his intermediary.

The lower-level judicial career pattern described here is likely
to be found in many civil courts of first instance as well as the
criminal courts. Municipal court justices, magistrates, justices of

the peace, county court judges, and the like are typical judicial careers of this stratum.

The Middle Level career pattern includes judges who are generally in the intermediate appellate courts of the country. This stratum of the judicial career is considered a reward, by way of promotion, for loyalty, service, and efficiency. The judges in these courts are usually selected by the governor of the state, subject to the approval of the legislature or some other body. The personnel are typically men (very few women ever serve as appellate judges) whose career pattern would include graduation from a law school which is above the level of the part-time "factory" but nevertheless not usually an elite school. As a lawyer the judge is likely to have had a moderately successful and discriminating practice, more dignified than the "ambulance chasing" of a negligence practice, but not necessarily with one of the major law firms. He very often combines a good sense of party politics with an intellectual flair in his work. In a word, he is usually more literate than his lower-level brethren; there is a strong likelihood he completed his B.A. work before going on to law school; perhaps he has even published in a scholarly journal. In any event, recruitment at this level is likely to be from among lower-level judges who not only have served the party well but have shown astuteness and imagination. The latter qualities are no guarantee of advancement, however, because the whole system of judicial career recruitment is so intimately related to the vicissitudes of precinct level politics that formal—or informal—criteria of selection may often be quite meaningless.

The Upper Level judge is likely to have come from an elite family and have been graduated from one of the "national" law schools. "National" law schools are those university schools that have established unqualified reputations for the high intellectual quality of their graduates and the strong faculties they have attracted for generations. They are the training ground for large numbers of the nation's political and business elites. The social frills of the undergraduate school are absent, the emphasis is on serious work, the alternative is failure. The leading schools are the Ivy League law schools, Yale, Harvard, and Columbia. There follow Cornell, Pennsylvania, Michigan, and Chicago.

The upper-level judge probably came from a major law firm and held a relatively important political office before being elevated to the bench. These judges are frequently prime candidates for the Supreme Court of the United States, which throughout its history has consisted mainly of those recruited from the "rich and well born." Only a very few persons of humble origin have ever become Supreme Court justices.[6]

Every law professor privately yearns for an upper-level judicial post as the capstone of his career, although professors are only infrequently designated for this office, which at the state level is generally elective. Although many upper-level judges have distinguished themselves as legal scholars, having published in the legal journals and in other scholarly journals, for the most part they are politically well connected and sophisticated in the vagaries of political life. Often they are simply possessed of great personal wealth and political influence and are otherwise prosaic and pedestrian.

It is interesting that judges at this level and at the lower trial and appellate levels are supposed to have virtually divorced themselves from the hurly-burly of political life. Indeed, Canon 28 of the Canons of Judicial Ethics of the American Bar Association forbids his engagement in any form of partisan politics—except in connection with his own candidacy for a judicial office. This canon is probably violated more than any other, especially at the lower level where there is a continuing contact with "politically visible" lawyers in the criminal court.

There are of course many judges whose particular career line may not fit any of the foregoing patterns. But it is clear that the "grand tradition" judge, the aloof, brooding, charismatic figure in the Old Testament tradition, is hardly a real figure. The reality is the working judge who must be politician, administrator, bureaucrat, and lawyer in order to cope with a crushing calendar of cases. A Metropolitan Court judge might well ask, "Did John Marshall or Oliver Wendell Holmes ever have to clear a calendar like mine?" The Metropolitan Court judge who sits in a court of original jurisdiction, in his role as trial judge, arbiter, sentencer, and awarder, cannot avoid the legal, interpersonal, and emotional dynamics of the small group of court regulars and those hangers-on who are inevitably present in a criminal court. By way of contrast, the middle-level or upper-level appellate judge is far removed from the original dispute and is therefore relatively unconcerned with the interpersonal dynamics of a given case and the various parties connected with it. His major sources of contact with a particular issue are lifeless briefs and a trial record.

Metropolitan Court judges, although they are among the highest paid in the world and wield considerable power in their limited domain, nevertheless feel somewhat marginal. They consider their activity to be peripheral to that of their civil court colleagues, and often they wistfully contrast the social importance of their work to that of the civil courts. They understand, however, that the bench and bar view them and the practitioners in their court as part of the least desirable aspect of law practice. The great intellectual challenges, and the arena in which the movers and shakers of our society operate, are thought to be in the civil courts. Metropolitan Court judges will recount fondly their exploits on those occasions when they have sat as civil judges, jousting with socially important litigants and their attorneys. One of them, speaking of his moment of glory in the civil court, related that attorneys were much impressed with the legally sophisticated manner in which he disposed of complex issues—and that he "really belonged" in the civil court.

SOCIO-DEMOGRAPHIC VARIABLES IN RECRUITMENT

By the time he has been elected to the bench, the mean age of a Metropolitan Court judge is fifty-one years. Retirement is mandatory at seventy. In the more than two hundred years of its existence, Metropolitan Court has never had a woman judge.

Of the nine justices who regularly sit in Metropolitan Court, only one is a graduate of a "national" law school; the others are graduates of part-time, proprietary, or "factory" types of schools.[7] Three of the nine justices completed their baccalaureate work before going to law school. In so far as their legal education was concerned, its course content did little to prepare them for their actual functions on the bench. Virtually all courses in most law schols are of the "bread and butter" variety, directed toward the candidate passing the bar examination of the particular state. Only rarely do they concern themselves with the serious issues of law administration, and virtually never do they deal with the social and economic implications of law and legal decision-making. As a result, there is no formal, systematic body of knowledge in legal education which can form the minimum requisite for a judicial career. Metropolitan Court judges—and most criminal court judges—are therefore, for the most part, poorly equipped to deal with the role challenges, dilemmas, and problems which they confront on the bench. A thorough knowledge of the criminal law is only rudimentary knowledge in the context of the onerous demands made by the criminal court bench.

Because he is ill-equipped to be a sophisticated decision-maker in a job that requires decision-making daily and routinely, and at the same time requires him to be an administrator, manager, and overseer, the judge must lean heavily on the services of others. As a consequence, Metropolitan Court justices, when they are initially appointed, are "broken in" by court clerks and other civil service functionaries who socialize them toward the "practical" goals and requirements of the court organization. This socialization is in fact actively sought by the judges in order to make their own work lives easier and to assuage their personal insecurities. As a matter of organizational and personal practicality, regardless of their individual predilections, they learn to accept and internalize the routineering and ritualism of their socializers.

Three of the nine justices in Metropolitan Court had prior judicial experience in courts of inferior criminal jurisdiction. In addition, the only justice who attended a national law school (whom we shall hereinafter refer to as Judge A) had some experience in a lower civil court. All had a history of extensive political activity and close clubhouse ties, four having served briefly as assistant district attorneys in the office of the prosecutor. All had engaged in private law practice for periods ranging from six to twenty years, and they had taken on some "criminal work" as part of their practice. None was employed by a major "Wall Street" type of law firm; instead they were associates or partners in small or medium-sized firms whose major practice was in the lower-level courts. They all had a moderate income from practice, although two of the judges possessed inherited wealth and were persons of financial means apart from their law practice. The other seven were never able to support more than an upper middle-class life style—and that rather precariously.

Intellectually, none was outstanding, except possibly Judge A, who was nevertheless only an average student at the Ivy League law school he attended. None possessed remarkable talents, although Judge X liked to sculpt. None was an outstanding lawyer or even a noted political figure before his elevation to judicial office. But they were noted as assiduous, loyal, and reliable party workers who made considerable contributions of time and money to their respective political clubs. The first political reward for their services was a law clerkship, an assignment to the office of the district attorney, or some minor court post. Judge A was most fortunate in having personal wealth and in beginning his judicial career as a lower civil court justice.

All the justices are sons of professional, proprietor, medium-sized mercantile or managerial fathers. Except for Justice J, the only Negro, they are all second- or third-generation Americans. Political leaders apparently endorse the idea that the bench's ethnic and religious composition, writ large, should be the same as the electorate's. The Metropolitan Court bench consists of four Catholics, two Protestants, and three Jews. For several decades there has always been at least one Negro justice in the court—an obvious token, because the court's geographic jurisdiction includes a substantial Negro population. The Catholic justices include three Irish and one Italian, which indicates the still strong dominance by Irish groups in the church, whose political influence is acknowledged by all the political professionals in Metropolitan Court to be considerable.

There is a continuing popular belief that the field of politics is an important exception to class rigidities and distinctions in America, that it still offers greater chances for social mobility than any other activity. But the experience of Metropolitan Court judges would belie this part of the American Dream. Seven of the judges are drawn from middle- and upper middle-class backgrounds. The fathers of the justices were at least as successful as their sons, although perhaps they did not have as high prestige. Only one justice, Judge X, is the son of a former city official, who is reputed to have acquired the family fortune in the course of his civic duties. Justice A, the other judge of considerable means, derived his wealth from his father's successful mercantile venture.

JUDICIAL DECISION-MAKING AND ANOMIE

Observers have used several frames of reference to try to explain the basis for judicial decision-making, the most fundamental aspect of the judge's job. These range from exploring the judge's personality [8] to applying small group theory, game theory, and a scale analysis of judicial voting behavior.[9] Indeed, the disciplined effort to identify the decision process with mathematical precision has been dubiously labeled "jurimetrics." [10]

One of the more significant variables in judicial decision-making is the level of the court. Upper-level judges are more scrupulously concerned with the niceties of legalism, for they do not face the voluminous case pressure and daily administrative tensions of the lower courts. Their distance from the persons involved in the case and the point of origin of the issues allows them to be sage-like, rather than bureaucratic and instrumental.

Similarly, political pressures—visible and invisible—will manifest themselves. Even though there may be no pressures on specific cases, the judge may not wish to offend those who have contributed to his past or may control his future when he comes up for reappointment or renomination. Only federal judges and some higher appellate state justices are appointed for life and are thus presumably above political pressures, but even they may be interested in being promoted. Inasmuch as most judgeships are often political rewards, there is likely to be an assumption of repayment by the judge for the reward. It may be in the form of judicial sympathy for the interests of the sponsors or former associates of the judge when litigation involving such interests comes before him. The judges of Metropolitan Court, being elected for a term of years and not for life, must always maintain a keen sensitivity to the desires, requirements, and interests of their political sponsors. In fact, the "easy" decision is the one that is politically inspired.

Of course, a judge's social biography will affect his decisions. Even the kind of law school he attended, or the nature of his practice before his judicial career, are elements in judicial decision-making. A judge who has come from a corporate or a commercial civil practice may have an entirely different decision pattern than one who has devoted much of his prior practice to criminal law and negligence. And class factors will have been a strong influence in determining the kind of practice the judge had. Indeed, sometimes a judge may react against his past as a criminal lawyer by being extremely harsh and punitive with the kinds of criminals he used to defend. This is the case with at least one well-known judge in the Metropolitan Court system.

The non-rational aspect of judicial decision-making may be best summed up by the confessional statement of one of America's leading contributors to jurisprudence, Chancellor James Kent. He indicated well over a century ago, in explaining how he reached a decision, that ". . . I might once in a while be embarrassed by a technical rule, but I almost always found principles suited to my view of the case . . ." [11] Even the much revered Oliver Wendell Holmes has indicated that "a decision is the unconscious result of instinctive prejudices and inarticulate connections . . ." and "even the prejudices which judges share with their fellow men have a good deal more to do than the syllogism in determining the rules by which men should be governed." [12]

Legal literature for the most part deals with the problems of judicial decision-making at the appellate level. At the level of Metropolitan Court the matter is much more complex because of the incredibly greater number of decisions that must be made, the greater variety of publics that must be served by the judge, and his greater anxiety because the legal rules themselves do not furnish adequate guidelines for his behavior. For example, if the Metropolitan Court judges were to permit themselves to be bound by statutory provisions for sentencing procedures, they would meet head on many groups in and out of the court who have vested interests in mitigating sentences and other rules. The judicial ambivalence toward rules is also apparent in connection with institutionalized evasions of the Canons of Judicial Ethics, especially Canon 14 requiring that "a judge should not be swayed by partisan demands," and Canon 28 forbidding his participation in politics except in connection with his own election. He cannot really adhere to these rules because every day he must respond to political commitments. Clubhouse lawyers are part of a constant procession of visitors to the judge's chambers, where there is frequent negotiation over plea and sentence.

Metropolitan Court judges rationalize their more obvious violations of the canons in terms of "community service" and "concern with social problems." They are caught in a bind which, by the nature of their office, compels them to behave with bureaucratic concern for production, efficient administration, and dispassionate enforcement of rules—and at the same time to be instruments of their political benefactors' particularistic designs and concerns.

Another aspect of the anomic character of the judge's conduct is reflected in the reluctance to place an individual on probation if he has been convicted after a jury trial. The justices in Metropolitan Court from time to time publicly affirm the importance of the jury trial as a central element of justice and due process. But privately, in their decision-making process, they will as a rule deny a probation disposition to a jury-convicted offender. In fact, the judges, the district attorney, and the probation report will, upon sentence of such an individual, explicitly note that "the defendant has caused the state to go to the expense of a trial." In 1962 the Metropolitan Court probation division investigated 3,643 out of 4,363 cases processed that year. (See Table 1.) Of the number investigated, 1,125 were placed on probation; all but three of these had pleaded guilty *before* trial.

Lower-level judges, in their decision-making and administrative conduct, are much more visible than are their appellate colleagues in the middle and upper courts. In a study of thirty appellate judges, three of whom were from federal courts and the others from various state superior courts, the judges were asked to define the least favorable aspects of their work. Two-thirds said isolation was the least favorable aspect of being an appellate judge. "I am segregated from the political, social, and economic arenas of life in which our destinies are shaped," was a comment that tended to summarize other similar comments. Two judges responded simply with one word, "Loneliness." Another judge deplored his "lack of personal contact with the litigants, witnesses, and others who play a part in each case." [13] With judges in Metropolitan Court, the situation is reversed. Here the justices are able to diffuse the anxieties and responsibilities of the decision-making process. As in any other bureaucracy, in the lower-level court the scope of decision-making is limited. Because there is perhaps even greater anxiety generated in the criminal court, the Metropolitan Court judges make an even more active effort than is usual in a bureaucracy to diffuse responsibility and authority. They simply are reluctant to carry the entire burden, and unlike the appellate courts, there are ample intermediaries and groups who can be invoked to share in the responsibilities which are ultimately those of the judge. Reluctant to shoulder the decision-making burden, and ambivalent toward formal rules and criteria which may interfere with his informal relations with political benefactors, lawyers, and other court personnel, the judge tailors each decision to suit his own needs. Thus for different decisions the judge will involve different court personnel, to diffuse responsibility and at the same time alleviate his own formal obligations.

Three fundamentally separate areas of decision-making show how the process in Metropolitan Court is anything but Solomon-like. While it is bureaucratic in terms of its rationality, it also involves the informal relations characteristic of that form of social organization. Thus, for example, one of the administrative functions of Metropolitan Court judges is budget-making. The formal structure of the court's fiscal personnel will be involved in the mechanical aspects of drawing up the budget. But specific, politically visible personnel, will counsel them informally as to the actual distribution of funds in a manner which will most effectively contribute to organizational discipline, morale, and control. The Metropolitan Court judges review the final distribution only in the most perfunctory, ministerial manner, for it represents decisions actually arrived at by others. What on the surface appears to be an administrative delegation based on the expertise and superior knowledge of those consulted, is in reality an effort at diffusion of decision-making responsibility. It is also a subtle design for the internal distribution of patronage and rewards to subordinates for continued loyalty to the judges.

A second area of decision-making in which the judge is supposed to have a major role, but which he relinquishes in large measure, is as overseer of the nature of the guilty plea which an accused offers before trial. Metropolitan Court judges are largely content to "pass the buck" to the district attorney who will frame the nature of the lesser plea to be accepted. Traditional judicial formulations would require the judge to act as an instrument of the whole community in reviewing the propriety of an accepted lesser plea. But here too Metropolitan Court judges have abdicated and prefer to ratify the plea negotiated by the district attorney, the defense counsel, and sometimes even the police. While the judge may have the right to reject a given plea, he rarely does so.

Although Metropolitan Court procedures are highly rational, it is not surprising to see the frequent number of spontaneous, last-minute, private conferences at the judge's bench in which minor details of a lesser plea are ironed out. Too often a judge has not been privy to the details of a negotiated plea. There is a fairly typical scene in which a judge has to muster all the authority of his office to smooth out a badly staged "cop-out ceremony." The judge must redirect the scene for the record, so that the plea will stand and the court can proceed to other matters. The following is an exact transcript of such an incident:

THE CLERK OF THE COURT: John Dukes, Edward Cash and James Sidwell, to the bar, Dukes and Cash on bail, Sidwell from the pen.

(Whereupon, the defendants were duly arraigned at the bar for pleading.)

THE CLERK OF THE COURT: Is your name John Dukes?

DEFENDANT DUKES: Yes.

THE CLERK OF THE COURT: Is Mr. McManus, who is present in court, your lawyer?

DEFENDANT DUKES: Yes, sir.

THE CLERK OF THE COURT: Now is your name Edward Cash?

DEFENDANT CASH: Yes.

THE CLERK OF THE COURT: Is Mr. Clover, who is present in the court, your lawyer?

DEFENDANT CASH: Yes.

THE CLERK OF THE COURT: And is your name James Sidwell?

DEFENDANT SIDWELL: Yes, it is.

THE COURT: Second call on Sidwell. (Sidwell's case is momentarily laid aside, his lawyer not being present.)

THE CLERK OF THE COURT: Now Dukes and Cash, each of you is indicted charged with the crimes of robbery in the first degree, etc.

(Whereupon, there was a conference at the bench, off the record and out of the hearing of the defendants, between the court, Mr. Weisbord, the assistant district attorney, and Messrs. McManus and Clover, counsel for the defendants Dukes and Cash, after which the following proceedings took place on the record in open court):

MR. MCMANUS: If your Honor pleases, the defendant John Dukes desires to plead guilty, as charged, in each and every count in the indictment.

THE COURT: John Dukes, do you wish to plead guilty to the crimes of robbery in the first degree, the first count, grand larceny in the first degree, the second count, assault in the second degree, the third count in the indictment?

DEFENDANT DUKES: Yes, I do.

THE COURT: And are you guilty of the crimes charged therein?

DEFENDANT DUKES: Yes.

THE COURT: Do you admit, by your plea of guilt, that in _____ County, on May 23, 1964, in the vicinity of Texarkana Avenue at 2nd Street, about 4:10 A.M., you unlawfully took certain property owned by Nelson Stanley, having a value of about one hundred seventy dollars, from the person or in the presence of Nelson Stanley but against his will, by means of force or violence or fear of immediate injury to his person, and were you at the time aided, that is, assisted in the commission of this robbery by your co-defendants?

DEFENDANT DUKES: *No, sir.*

THE COURT: Did you perpetrate this robbery alone?

DEFENDANT DUKES: Well, I was alone. It was a crowd of fifteen people there, and I went to the crowd of fifteen, and I picked the wallet up off the ground. I went to the defense of the complainant but by me being in the crowd he picked me out.

THE COURT: I don't quite understand.

DEFENDANT DUKES: It was only supposed to be ninety dollars involved.

THE COURT: I am not concerned about the amount of money involved. I am concerned only about the circumstance under which you got possession of this money. Did you take it by force from the person or the possession of this victim, Nelson Stanley?

DEFENDANT DUKES: *No, sir.*

THE COURT: Did you threaten him?

DEFENDANT DUKES: *No, sir.*

THE COURT: Then I cannot accept a plea to the indictment, Mr. McManus. Do you want to confer with your client?

DEFENDANT DUKES: Somebody else took the wallet. I picked the wallet up.

THE COURT: Did this someone else help you in the commission of a robbery on Nelson Stanley? Mr. Dukes, I am not asking you to name anyone. I am asking you whether or not you, either alone or with someone else, acting in concert with you, committed a robbery on Nelson Stanley?

DEFENDANT DUKES: Yes.

THE COURT: Now, a moment ago you said you came to his aid, you came to help him. Was that the truth when you made that statement, or were you lying to me?

DEFENDANT DUKES: (No response.)

THE COURT: Mr. McManus, I am going to suggest that you confer with your client.

MR. MCMANUS: *I have conferred, your Honor. You know, sometimes, when it comes to this point, they somehow or other gag, so to speak, to use a vulgar expression* [our italics], but what confused him I think was the amount of money. He claims it was ninety dollars.

THE COURT: I wouldn't care if it was two dollars. The amount of money involved is no element of the crime. I am going to start all over again. I want you to be truthful, do you understand?

DEFENDANT DUKES: Yes, your Honor.

THE COURT: Do you want me to take this plea? Do you still wish to plead guilty to the three counts in the indictment?

DEFENDANT DUKES: Yes, sir.

THE COURT: That is, robbery in the first degree, grand larceny in the first degree and assault in the second degree?

DEFENDANT DUKES: Yes, sir.

THE COURT: Is that your wish?

DEFENDANT DUKES: That's right.

THE COURT: By your plea of guilty, do you admit that on May 23, 1964, at about 4:10 in the morning, in the vicinity of Texarkana Avenue and 2nd Street, you, together with one or more other persons who aided you in the commission of this crime, unlawfully took certain moneys owned by Nelson Stanley from his presence or from his person but against his will, by means of force or violence, or by fear of immediate injury to his person?

DEFENDANT DUKES: Yes, sir. Me alone.

THE COURT: Now I am going to ask you this question again. Was there another person, one or more persons, who assisted you? I am not asking you to name who they are. I am merely asking you were you assisted in the commission of this robbery by one or more other persons who were actually present at the time? Now can you answer that question.

DEFENDANT DUKES: Yes, sir, there was more people present.

THE COURT: I didn't ask you if there were more people present watching.

DEFENDANT DUKES: Yes, sir.

THE COURT: Now, look, Dukes, you understand me when I question you.

DEFENDANT DUKES: Yes, your Honor.

THE COURT: You understand that a robbery may be committed by one or it may be committed by two, three or more persons, is that right?

DEFENDANT DUKES: Yes.

THE COURT: Now, you are pleading to an indictment which charges that you, together with others, acting in concert with you, committed a robbery. Is that the fact?

DEFENDANT DUKES: I didn't understand that, your Honor. Yes.

THE COURT: Edward Cash, you are represented by Mr. Clover?

DEFENDANT CASH: Yes, your Honor.

THE COURT: You are not prepared today to make any disposition, is that right, Mr. Clover?

MR. CLOVER: That's correct, your Honor.

THE COURT: Have you a bail application?

MR. CLOVER: Yes, I do.

THE COURT: What is your application?

MR. CLOVER: My application is to reduce the bail in the sum of fifteen hundred dollars.

THE COURT: I have conferred with the District Attorney, and that is consented to. Bail in the case of Edward Cash is now fixed at fifteen hundred dollars. Remand the defendant. Now, Dukes, do you want to start all over again?

DEFENDANT DUKES: Yes, sir.

THE COURT: And I will speak slowly. Your lawyer made an offer to plead guilty, on your behalf, to the entire indictment—that's three counts—which charges you with the following crimes: robbery in the first degree, grand larceny in the first degree and assault in the second degree. Do you wish to plead guilty to those crimes?

DEFENDANT DUKES: Yes, sir.

THE COURT: By your pleas of guilt, do you admit that on May 23, 1964, at about four o'clock in the morning, in the vicinity of Texarkana and 2nd Street, you stole—stole—certain moneys, that is, you unlawfully took this money from the person and owned by Nelson Stanley from his person or in his presence, but against his will, by means of force or violence or fear of immediate injury to his person, and were you at the time aided in any degree whatsoever in the commission of this robbery by one or more other persons who were actually present at the time with you?

DEFENDANT DUKES: Yes, sir.

THE COURT: Now, is that a truthful answer?

DEFENDANT DUKES: Yes, sir.

THE COURT: Has your lawyer informed you that you have a prior felony conviction?

DEFENDANT DUKES: That's right.

THE COURT: And that I will be required to sentence you on any of these three counts as a second felony offender? Are you aware of that? Has he outlined that to you?

DEFENDANT DUKES: Yes.

THE COURT: Has anyone given you any kind of a promise whatsoever as to the nature of the sentence I would impose upon you in order to induce you to plead guilty?

DEFENDANT DUKES: No, sir.

THE COURT: Take the plea.

THE CLERK OF THE COURT: John Dukes, the Court now informs you that if you have been previously convicted of a crime, that fact may be established, and if you plead guilty or are convicted under this indictment, you will be subject to the additional or different punishment prescribed or authorized by reason of such prior conviction. Do you understand that, Mr. Dukes?

DEFENDANT DUKES: Yes.

THE CLERK OF THE COURT: Now, Mr. Dukes, again, with your lawyer present, Mr. McManus, I again inform you that if you have previously been convicted of a crime, that fact may be established, and if you plead guilty or are convicted under this indictment, you will be subject to the different or additional punishment prescribed or authorized by reason of this prior conviction. Do you understand that now?

DEFENDANT DUKES: Yes, I do.

THE CLERK OF THE COURT: You do understand it?

DEFENDANT DUKES: Yes.

THE CLERK OF THE COURT: Now do you plead guilty to the crimes of robbery in the first degree, the first count of this indictment, and grand larceny in the second degree, the second count of this indictment, and assault in the second degree, the third count of this indictment, to cover the indictment? Is that your plea?

DEFENDANT DUKES: Yes.

In this not unusual instance, the judge had to reorient a defendant who had obviously begun to have second thoughts about his guilty plea. The judge carefully reconstituted the defendant's thought processes so that they would more precisely fit the desired "guilty" mold. Here the judge took an active, assertive role, lending the resources of his office to seal the "bargain" of the plea and to quickly place a stamp of legality and finality upon it.

It is, however, in the area of sentencing that judges show

their greatest ambivalence and inconsistency. Some men may glory in being a criminal court judge, but others are entirely ambivalent about the responsibilities of sentencing their fellow men to prison or death. The latter description for the most part fits the Metropolitan Court judges. They have therefore arranged for elaborate probation and psychiatric reports which they can "lean on" in deciding an otherwise difficult case. Where there are strong political considerations, or where there is a mandatory penalty with little exercise of discretion possible, judicial decision-making is circumscribed. But often the judge is confronted with a situation that offers too few or too weak criteria for decision. He will then deliberately involve probation and psychiatric reports or a district attorney's recommendations to diffuse responsibility or to mitigate his own anxieties. And what *appears* to be a group decision is also more palatable in organizational life to client, workers, and the publics concerned. The bureaucratic admonition of "cover yourself" applies as well to the judge as to any other individual in the organizational world. The group decision functions not only to conceal individual mediocrity but can also be pointed to as evidence of profound efforts to individualize, and at the same time make the administration of justice more uniform and equitable.

PATTERNS OF JUDICIAL ROLE PERFORMANCE

As in the case of any other role, there are minimal standards which any judge must meet, and no two judges perform their judicial role obligations in precisely identical fashion. As a source of career and ego satisfaction, the bench furnishes a rich variety of possibilities. Further, organizational requirements appear to harness and exploit the idiosyncracies of individual judges for organizational ends. The distribution of the Metropolitan Court workload is evidence of this feature of organizational life. The judges and their retinue are loath to discuss the distribution of the work load, and the reason for this becomes apparent in Table 8. There were 4,363 cases processed in 1962. Each of the nine judges were rotated among the various "parts" of the court and thus, theoretically at least, had equal access to the court's case load.

Table 8: Distribution of Metropolitan Court judicial work load in 1962

No. of cases disposed of	Judge	Per cent of total caseload
1519	A	34.8
112	L	2.6
198	M	4.5
1326	X	30.4
287	J	6.6
132	P	3.0
147	K	3.4
229	D	5.2
413	G	9.5
TOTAL 4363		**100.0%**

It is readily apparent that two judges, A and X, were responsible for disposing of more than half the court's case load during 1962. Further, the differing participation in the work load reflects the individual performance patterns of the judges. The intellectual and emotional characteristics of each judge are structurally used to advance organization drives, needs, and ends.

In the judges' actual performances, discerned in part from their work load activity, six major judicial role patterns may be perceived.

1. "Intellectual"–Scholar } "Workhorses" of
2. Routineer–Hack } the court
3. Political Adventurer–Careerist
4. Judicial Pensioner
5. "Hatchet Man"
6. "Tyrant"–"Showboat"–"Benevolent Despot"

Actually, the Metropolitan Court during its modern history has always had one or two justices who have carried a substantial portion of the work load. The other justices may secretly chafe under this, but they are remarkably acquiescent about a situation that relieves them of a good deal of burden and responsibility. And as a matter of organizational practicality, in advancing goals of maximum production, it is perhaps more efficient to narrow the circle of individuals whose mission it will be to accomplish these ends.

Judges A and X, who are the workhorses of the court, perform their respective organizational roles in entirely different ways. Judge A, a graduate of an Ivy League law school, is the bench member with intellectual and scholarly leanings but with a great personal need to be continuously involved in the fray of "wheeling and dealing." A not uncommon sight in his courtroom is the tumultuous scene of a trial in progress, interrupted so that Judge A can accept fifteen to twenty lesser pleas of guilty; hear motions on various matters affecting cases before him; sentence several cases previously heard; or consult with lawyers, probation officers, or members of the district attorney's staff. The other justices and members of the court community refer to Judge A's courtroom as a three-ring circus. His fellow judges view with consternation and misgivings the fact that he frequently works on Saturdays, Sundays, holidays, and at odd hours of the night. His passion for work is regarded with suspicion, but all in the court community admit that Judge A "gets results." He is sought after by defense counsel because it is generally known that Judge A is an eminently "practical" man who is more than willing to compromise in return for a plea. He is also very sensitive to political cues, and his office has a veritable procession of individuals seeking his intervention, counsel, and assistance.

Possessed of personal charm, wit, and intelligence, Judge A sees his organizational role as that of maximizing production, even if traditional rules have to be bent. Often he uses his reputation for leniency and "practicality" as a means of disposing of the welter of cases which are for those very reasons funneled to him for disposition.

Judge X is a more traditional political figure on the bench. Like

Judge A he has inherited wealth. He is the son of a former important municipal official. Basically, his career aspirations are limited, but he greatly enjoys his work, which he is really incapable of handling in other than a routine fashion. His great production is a result of his easygoing, non-punitive attitude, coupled with his personal desire to make his mark in the organization. Because he is otherwise prosaic and pedestrian, other judges do not consider him as much of a threat as Judge A. The judgeship for him is simply a comfortable slot, a means of maintaining work and other ego needs which would not otherwise be available to him.

Judges G and J are extremely well connected politically, and so their lackluster performance in Metropolitan Court is of no consequence. As "political adventurer–careerist" types their incumbency will be short-lived; the bench is only a steppingstone to other political offices they desire. They have no profound interest in law, or for that matter in the administration of the criminal law. They are more concerned with building their personal and organizational empires elsewhere, and most of their efforts will be directed not toward cases that come before them but toward manipulating the organization for their own ends. At times they will try to develop favorable press publicity about themselves and their judicial careers, as part of their overall career plan. Of course, judges like this sometimes fail and find they have been consigned to a lower court career. The resulting bitterness and querulousness can transform them into "pensioners," "routineers," or "tyrants."

The "judicial pensioner" is a judge who has been rewarded rather late in his political life. He prefers to be left undisturbed, to spend as little of his time as possible in court; he wants an almost anonymous existence. He takes virtually no interest in the administrative activities of the court. It is as though he were already retired. Judges L, M, and P have had long, active political careers at the clubhouse level, and they have been elevated to the bench either to discharge a political obligation or to get them safely out of the way.

The "hatchet man" role is often played by a member of the bench who has previously had a career in the office of the district attorney. He has close ties to that office, the political clubhouse, and other areas of power in municipal government. His role and function in the court are to take care of those cases involving special difficulty because of their "public" nature—in other words, those cases characterized by crimes of delict, malfeasance, or breach of trust committed by public officials and petty civil servants which place the municipal administration on the defensive. Also grist for the "hatchet man's" mill are those accused persons who have refused to cooperate with the prosecuting authorities, or whose cases involve special features of scandal or opprobrium and are being avidly watched by the news media. It is his function to stage manage an impression of swift justice—impassively, clinically, and uniformly administered.

The "tyrant"–"showboat"–"benevolent despot" is usually the same judge on different occasions. He is a deeply hostile, frustrated, ambition-ridden individual who has been defeated in his career aspirations. He is at a dead end and knows it. Possessed of an unbounding contempt and scorn for others, his grandiosity is incredible. He is the terror of his courtroom. Lawyers, accused persons, and probation officers fear him and loathe him. District attorneys simply abide his irascible, acidulous, querulous, surly manner. The social context of the courtroom provides an outlet for the kind of sadistic exhibitionism that is characteristic of this judicial role. Largely rejected by his colleagues, this egocentric individual exploits his judicial post as a vehicle to attract the attention of the press. He glories in the publicity he receives, even if it is negative. His harshness and intemperance are occasionally relieved by acts of charity and forbearance, which he is quick to exploit through publicity in the news media.

The most destructive aspect of his conduct, however, is the way he meets his professional and legal obligations in the courtroom itself. Here he completely dominates the proceedings and manipulates them toward his own ends—or what he perceives to be truth and reality. He has complete control over the court stenographer, virtually furnishing the material the stenographer is to include or exclude from the record in connection with his own comments and statements—which may have been improper. He manipulates juries through smiles, smirks, and unrecorded off-the-cuff comments which may tend to discredit a witness or a defendant's testimony during a trial. He intimidates defendants, privately threatens lawyers. Thus, cloaked in organizational authority and appearing to be performing important activities in furtherance of organizational goals, he is meeting the needs of personal pathology.

In large measure, however, all the judicial types, despite the different character of their performances, contribute to the court organization as a functioning mechanism. The division of labor in the court is not as random and fortuitous as it may appear. Each judicial role type is cultivated, for each contributes in his own way to the total institutional arrangement. Individual needs are capitalized and rationalized in the service of the court organization. As long as individual aberrations do not materially interfere with the achievement of organization objectives, they will be permitted to proceed undisturbed.

7

Probation and psychiatry

> "I'll be judge, I'll be jury," said cunning old Fury;
> "I'll try the whole cause, and condemn you to death."
> —Lewis Carroll, *Alice in Wonderland*

We shall not be concerned, except in an incidental way, with probation as a procedure for the supervision of one who is found guilty of a crime and then released by the court; nor shall we discuss psychiatry as therapy. Instead, we shall consider psychiatry and probation as administrative devices for evaluating and disposing of an offender in the organizational setting of a criminal court.

Over the years there has been considerable discussion as to whether probation or psychiatry, depending as they do on a particular kind of rapport between the client and practitioner, can ever be effective. Attempts at diagnosis or treatment, probation or psychiatry, in the authoritative setting of a court have not on the whole offered encouraging results. In so far as the scope and function of the criminal court are concerned, the diagnostic aspect of these two services is the more significant. For it is the diagnostic, evaluative features of probation and psychiatry that are invoked by the court more than any other function. In most other organizations, in fact, psychiatrists spend most of their time with diagnosis and evaluation, with little time left for treatment, even if that should be part of their duties.

Probation workers think they are guided essentially by the precepts of social work, a discipline grounded in the work of Freud, Adler, and Rank. The worker must understand himself as well as his client in order to diagnose and evaluate properly. Although the origins of probation can be traced back to reprieves granted to offenders who could claim "benefit of clergy" in the thirteenth century,[1] modern probation theory and method are more intimately related with developments in social work. The professional role model of the probation officer is the social worker, but for both these groups psychiatry serves as their occupational model and fund of knowledge.

The modern function of probation, as epitomized in the presentence investigation report, draws upon social work's early concept of social diagnosis. This in turn grows out of the social worker's "need to know" in order to "work out" a problem, to apprehend and develop a line of orientation in connection with a client's dilemma. Thus social diagnosis is "the attempt to arrive at as exact a definition as possible of the social situation and personality of a given client." [2] To arrive at a diagnosis the worker uses raw material and data about the client gleaned from other social agencies, relatives, friends, schools, employers, public records, medical records, and any other such sources as may be available. He then interprets and analyzes the information and decides upon the nature of the client's problems and their probable solutions. Diagnosis and classification based on intimate knowledge of the client's personality are central to what has been called the diagnostic school of social work.[3]

It is this approach, then, that has been appropriated as the basic element of the probation pre-sentence investigation which precedes the final disposition of a case in the criminal court. This fundamental objective of probation is stated by one worker in the field as follows:

> Even before probation had been absorbed into the generic social work movement, the investigation report had come to be the repository for all biographical data needed not only for supervision in the free community but also for planning and executing rehabilitative programs for offenders committed to prisons and reformatories. Thus, the investigation (diagnostic) process, became as important as the rehabilitation (treatment) process. It is, in fact, of greater importance, since it is the bedrock of treatment. Quantitatively, it is now the most significant part of all probation work.[4]

Pre-sentence reports usually include such items as the details of the immediate offense, as obtained from the district attorney and the police; the defendant's prior criminal history, if any; the attitude of the complainant in the case; and a personal history of the defendant in terms of early development, employment, education, and personal data in connection with family or marriage. The report will include information about his mental and physical condition, probably furnished by a hospital or a private psychiatrist. (Very few adult criminal courts in the country have their own resources to furnish this service.[5]) Many cases are processed for judicial disposition on the basis of criteria other than the pre-sentence investigation report. But in a substantial minority of cases the probation report becomes an important element in the decision-making process, if not the sole criterion on which the judge relies.

Indeed, in the very case in which the United States Supreme Court upheld the validity of the pre-sentence probation investigation as meeting the due process requirements of the Constitution, the defendant's life was at stake.[6] He had been convicted by a jury of the murder of a fifteen-year-old girl during a burglary. The jury recommended leniency, which in a murder case at that time permitted a judge to sentence a defendant to life imprisonment rather than death. But the judge ignored the jury's recommendation and sentenced the defendant to be executed. Among other grounds for his decision, the judge cited the negative contents of the pre-sentence investigation report as to the defendant's social history, including other crimes he was alleged to have committed. While the Supreme Court was aware that aspects of the pre-sentence investigation violate due process in that hearsay evidence is used, it nevertheless upheld the legal propriety of the pre-sentence procedure. Although the report contained material furnished by the police and others that was not presented in open court "on the record," and therefore was not available to cross-examination or denial by the accused or his counsel, the report was adjudged not to violate due process.

In upholding the validity of pre-sentence reports, the Supreme Court assumed that a probation department functions in an autonomous role, mediating impartially between the court and the defendant. In reality this is not at all the case. This ideal relationship does not exist anywhere in America. On the contrary, the budgetary procedures, the recruitment and supervision of personnel, the directives and procedures which control and channel the daily operations of a probation division all flow from the court structure, and probation personnel are only a part of it. A probation department's "independence" and "impartiality" are inevitably tainted by its involvement with the organizational motives and designs of the court itself.

While the pre-sentence probation investigation, based on a rationale of individualizing offenders, has been only recently accepted in the criminal court, psychiatry is an older and more firmly established part of the court system. Psychiatry's claims to validity in the criminal court setting go back to the ancient Hebrew and Roman cultures, when individuals who were obviously not oriented to the usual spheres of time, place, and identity were excused from criminal liability. Today in American criminal courts, psychiatrists are regularly asked to testify in connection with the so-called McNaghten rule. Stated quite simply, the rule established in 1843 in the English courts and adopted in most American states is as follows:

An individual is not criminally culpable if at the time he commits a crime he is "laboring under such defect of reason" as (a) not to know the nature and quality of his act; or (b) not to know his act was wrong. Although it was the "right-wrong" test of the McNaghten rule which brought psychiatry an active role in criminal trials, the growth of psychiatry as a discipline and as a social institution proliferated its functions in various administrative and institutional settings. Thus psychiatry performs a function in schools, factories, corporate executive suites, and non-judicial public agencies similar to its role in the criminal court. The psychiatrist is plainly an employee of the organization whose services and skills are invoked to render a decision or furnish a statement about the *present* mental state of the job applicant, the schoolteacher, the child, or any employee who has been "difficult."

In the criminal court, especially in those courts which employ psychiatrists as regular members of the court staff, they are called upon routinely to evaluate offenders. Their reports are often incorporated into the pre-sentence or even the pre-pleading investigation report submitted by the probation staff. In that function, the diagnostic procedures of psychiatry are used to determine the existence of a medically defined psychosis, as distinguished from the legalistic concept of "insanity" under the McNaghten rule. Thus psychiatry is administratively invoked at two important levels in the criminal court. In connection with the trial of an accused person, the psychiatrist may be called upon to offer expert testimony about the pre-existing mental condition of the defendant who asserts immunity on the grounds of his legal insanity at the time of the commission of the offense. The final decision as to the validity of such a claim, after psychiatric testimony for both sides has been heard, rests with the jury.

Of greater significance, however, is the role of psychiatry in routinely examining defendants either before or after a plea of guilty, to determine the *present* existence of a medically rather than a legally defined psychosis. What this amounts to is simply an *ex parte* report from the court's employee, the psychiatrist, to his principal, the court organization. There is no possibility of rebuttal, as there might ordinarily be during trial. At the very least, in a trial situation its adversary features would also include psychiatric testimony favorable to the accused's position. The psychiatric profession of course chafes under this situation. The spectacle of two or more qualified (and even at times eminent) psychiatrists making diametrically opposed statements in a courtroom about an accused's prior and present mental condition has been viewed with dismay by members of the profession. It has also helped to present psychiatry to the world as something other than a "science," despite its own science-building model and its claims of scientific impartiality.

The brutal fact, which every criminal lawyer learns early in his career, is that psychiatric testimony is for sale. Indeed, some important practitioners spend much of their time delivering courtroom testimony and acting as an expert witness for a fee. The entire glossary of psychiatry is available for purchase, not because of corruption but simply because of the incredible flexibility and vacuousness of its diagnostic labels and pigeonholes. These labels, which are drawn from such diverse linguistic frameworks as the mental hospital, psychoanalytic practice, the military service, the psychiatric clinic, and the child-guidance clinic, when employed in analyzing a defendant in a criminal case can be extremely damaging. As Thomas Szasz states, "It is significant that the nosological categories of Kraepelin, Bleuler, Freud, and Goldstein [continue] to be used. Each makes sense in the setting in which it originated. However, these categories have since been combined with one another, and are now used in every conceivable situation. Is it surprising then that our current psychiatric nosology is a modern Tower of Babel?" [7]

Judges are often delighted with the way in which a psychiatric label submitted in the course of a routine examination of an accused furnishes a neat "scientific" framework and rationale for a particular sentence or plea. Diagnostic language which in other frameworks of practice, time, and place means one thing, takes on an entirely condemnatory meaning in the criminal court. Thus, for example, a typically vague psychiatric label of "pathologic emotionality, inadequate and emotionally unstable type" presages the possibility of all kinds of judicial mischief toward an accused to whom it is applied. Judges often select disparate elements of a probation and psychiatric report to suit particular objectives they may have in mind. The disciplines of probation and psychiatry become the willing handmaidens of the court organization, for individual careers are too often wholly dependent upon the wielders of judicial power.[8]

Following are representative samples of complete diagnostic reports culled from over two thousand such reports issued by the psychiatric clinic of Metropolitan Court during the year 1964–1965.

This defendant is WITHOUT PSYCHOSIS and of borderline intelligence.

Defendant gives a history of impaired schooling, but formal psychologic testing excludes mental deficiency, revealing an I.Q. of 77, which classifies him as borderline.

There are no signs of serious personality disorder, and our diagnosis is ADYNAMIC, DULL TYPE WITH DRUG ADDICTION.

Physical examination reveals no significant findings, except for recent withdrawal symptoms due to drugs.

Respectfully submitted,

_____, M.D.

Psychiatrist-in-Charge

This defendant is WITHOUT PSYCHOSIS and estimated to be of low average intelligence.

Present examination reveals a SUGGESTIBLE PASSIVE TYPE of personality with DRUG ADDICTION.

Physical examination reveals needle marks of the left arm due to self-injection of drugs.

Respectfully submitted,

————————————, M.D.

Psychiatrist-in-Charge

This defendant is WITHOUT PSYCHOSIS and estimated to be of low average intelligence.

Defendant minimized his early difficulties and direct examination here reveals only an IMMATURE ADULT.

Physical examination reveals no significant findings.

Respectfully submitted,

————————————, M.D.

Psychiatrist-in-Charge

This defendant is not psychotic and is of average intelligence.

She admits to the present offense and gives what she believes are extenuating circumstances. She talks in quite a husky voice and states that twelve years ago she had polyps removed from her vocal chords and her speech is a result of this operation. She has apparently supported herself up to date and been fairly conformist up to date.

She is classified as an Aggressive and Self-Centered individual.

Physical is within normal limits.

Respectfully submitted,

————————————, M.D.

Psychiatrist-in-Charge

This defendant is WITHOUT PSYCHOSIS and is estimated to be within the normal range of intelligence.

Present examination indicated a diagnosis of INADEQUATE PERSONALITY WITH DRUG ADDICTION.

Physical examination revealed needle marks of both arms due to self-injection of drugs.

Respectfully submitted,

————————————, M.D.

Psychiatrist-in-Charge

This defendant is WITHOUT PSYCHOSIS and is of borderline intelligence.

Defendant gave a history of retardation in school and psychological testing here reveals an I.Q. of 74, which is a borderline rating.

Psychiatric examination indicates that he has a severe reading and writing disability but is not actually defective or certifiable to an institution. He is basically well motivated and seems to have associated with gangs recently due to reaction of inferiority.

Our diagnosis is AGGRESSION WITH REACTION TO INFERIORITY.

Physical examination reveals no significant findings.

Respectfully submitted,

_____, M.D.

Psychiatrist-in-Charge

This defendant is not psychotic and is of average intelligence.

She admits to the present offense and states that this shooting was the outgrowth of an argument. She adds that she and the complainant plan to be married in the near future despite the present events.

She is classified as an Aggressive and Self-Centered Individual with Aggression Released by Alcohol.

Physical within normal limits.

Respectfully submitted,

_____, M.D.

Psychiatrist-in-Charge

This defendant is WITHOUT PSYCHOSIS and is of borderline intelligence.

Present examination reveals little change since the previous examination here in 1957 and we are continuing the diagnosis of AGGRESSION IN REACTION TO INFERIORITY.

Physical examination reveals no significant findings.

Respectfully submitted,

_____, M.D.

Psychiatrist-in-Charge

Examination of this defendant indicates that he is without psychosis and of average intelligence.

At interview, he is seen to be quiet, soft spoken, composed, displaying little deep-seated sense of guilt and a rather self-indulgent and optimistic attitude. He apparently has been a generally industrious and responsible individual, though inclined to have somewhat relaxed ethical standards in regard to money matters. He gambles excessively, usually at the horse races, and will use various check writing and check kiting stratagems to handle present family expenses. Up to now, he has been able to make restitution through his good earning capacity and the assistance of his indulgent relatives.

Personality classification is best described as that of the Egocentric Type.

Physical examination is essentially negative. He has some scars of second-degree burns and corrective skin grafting procedures involving the left thigh and left leg. This is a result of a World War Two injury.

Respectfully submitted,

————————————————, M.D.

Senior Psychiatrist

This defendant is not psychotic and is of average intelligence. He was arrested on the premises and admits to the present offense.

In the past he has been a drug addict. He states that he did not return to drugs since leaving the penitentiary. This may or may not be true. He apparently makes his living as an apartment burglar.

He was examined in this Clinic in 1954 and has been in conflict with the law since his earliest youth.

He is classified as he previously has been. He is a Pathological Individual, Antisocial, with drug addiction. His arms bear the marks of this addiction. His physical examination is otherwise within normal limits.

Respectfully submitted,

————————————————, M.D.

Psychiatrist-in-Charge

It may readily be seen that by their cursory, capsule-like style the reports are rather glib evaluations which can serve as a convenient peg on which to base an often difficult judicial decision. Psychiatric labels in this context serve essential administrative needs, but stripped of their function as mere categories and scaled down to their predictive value they are quite crude and almost meaningless.

It is a settled matter of law that courts will not overturn an administrative agency's findings of fact. Such determinations are considered conclusive and final.[9] The basis for this view is the notion that the administrative agency possesses skills and technology which enable it to sort out conflicting claims and establish the "facts." Legalists assume that administrative agencies will act impartially, mediating dispassionately between their publics and the requirements of the state. It was this tacit notion which lay at the foundation of the Supreme Court's acceptance of pre-sentence probation investigations. But sociological knowledge of organizational realities introduces a note of skepticism into this idealized situation. As Paul Tappan has indicated:

> Judicious qualities of mind and judicial techniques of inquiry are not the rule among effective administrators who are bent upon speedy attainment of goals. There is little respect among them for "legalism," "technicality," "due process," or other obstructions to the exercise of power.[10]

Psychiatric clinics and probation bureaus are essentially fact-finding arms of the administrative agency that employs them. But their "findings" are seldom subject to review or close scrutiny. The instruments, procedures, and methods used by fact finders in an administrative agency should not proceed unchallenged indefinitely. The charisma of professional expertise, when routinized in an organizational setting, performing bureaucratic functions to further an organization's goals, often becomes hack-work. The absence of systematic inquiry and vigorous methodology calls into question the validity of the "facts" that are found. Regrettably, psychiatry and probation help to process a given case more "efficiently" and quite often are not related to finding the facts.

THE CIVIL SERVICE MALAISE

It is highly unlikely that a court's probation and psychiatric personnel originally set their sights on that sort of professional career. In Metropolitan Court the sixty probation officers, as well as the psychiatrists and clinical psychologists, had envisioned other jobs than those in which they find themselves. They have surrendered earlier illusions to accept the realities of limited career opportunities. They equate this lowering of their career sights, and the acceptance of their role as organizational instruments, with "emotional maturity" and "adult responsibility." Given to the patois of social work and psychiatry, they characterize their subservience to organizational demands as "dealing effectively with reality." Although their respective journals continue to support the myth of the free "professional" in bureaucracy, their lack of genuine professional status in the court is a constant source of personal anxiety, work alienation, and general dissatisfaction. This is especially true for the probation officer, which is undoubtedly the most marginal of the various occupational groupings.

Sixteen probation officers in Metropolitan Court, or approximately 25 per cent of the total, are graduates of schools of social work. The remainder have done graduate work in sociology, psychology, law, business administration, education, and nursing. The graduate social workers drifted from one low-paying private agency job to another before coming to Metropolitan Court. They say they realized they were "stepping down" in terms of their professional ideologies and skills, but they did so willingly and perhaps even eagerly. Apart from the "money" and "security" which all mentioned as the foremost reasons for coming to the court, most of the graduate social workers said they had become disenchanted with social work as a professional and intellectual enterprise. Probation supervisors found the professional social workers the most difficult personnel to "break in." These workers had great difficulty abandoning some of the more superficial professional characteristics that social work practice afforded, such as "professional supervision." What's more, probation, because of its authoritative and often punitive orientations, was initially offensive to the professional social worker, who had been trained in an entirely different ethos. In Metropolitan Court, however, attractive pay scales are the lure to keep even the most discontented social worker from leaving.

The recruitment of other probation workers in the court has been similar to that of the social workers. They had all drifted from one low-paying public or private job to another, they were disenchanted with their career, and they were attracted to probation by the possibility of job autonomy. For virtually all the probation staff, the major basis for recruitment is a conscious limitation of career aspiration in return for the civil service security of tenure. Very little is required of the individual by way of a creative or original performance. The more prosaic his functioning in compliance with organizational stereotypes, the more favorably he is regarded as a worker.

Personnel turnover, until recently, had been low. This may be the result not only of a favorable salary structure but also of the nature of probation as work experience. While work experience is transferable from one job location to another in most professions, such is not the case with probation. Outside the major urban areas, salaries and working conditions deteriorate. Further, each agency has its own set of work requisites, and "experience" as such does not count as much as in other occupations. Promotional opportunities are virtually nonexistent, for in many probation agencies higher administrative positions are filled largely through political recruitment. Where promotion to supervisory and administrative positions is subject to civil service procedures, it is infrequent and limited. Career escalation, if it is to take place at all, must occur within the extremely rigid and limited confines of a particular probation division. In most instances even the other positions in the court organization are not open to probation personnel as a promotion possibility or opportunity. This factor, coupled with the very limited transferability of skills or experience to other organizations, makes the work role of a probation officer a career dead end.

At one time in Metropolitan Court, as in many other probation departments, many of the jobs were filled by civil service–conscious Irish Catholics. This ethnic group had gravitated toward probation in the same manner that large numbers of them had traditionally filled other law enforcement positions. But as career opportunities and structural possibilities in other fields began to open up for them, college-educated Irish Catholics sought careers in other more rewarding areas. In keeping with the tradition of the lower ranks of civil service as a ladder of mobility into the middle class, the Jews followed the Catholics into the civil service milieu. Now both the Irish Catholics and the Jews are being rapidly replaced by Negroes and Puerto Ricans, as these groups produce their first significant crops of college graduates. As a consequence, approximately one-fourth of the staff of the probation division in Metropolitan Court is now Negroes and Puerto Ricans; the balance of the staff consists of an almost evenly distributed number of Irish and Italian Catholics, and Jews. In terms of social class, all were recruited from the lower- and lower middle-class, and one of their major sources of satisfaction is their belief that they have achieved some degree of social mobility, in contrast to their parents' status.

The greatest source of dissonance in their work lives is the tenuous and unrealistic nature of their asserted professionalism. Probation journals and probation workers' organizations emphasize the "professional" nature of probation work. Like the funeral director, the hospital administrator, the accountant, and the social worker, the probation officer has attempted to professionalize. But he has tried to do so by fiat rather than by developing a special body of technical knowledge. The self-image of the probation officer as a professional is seriously negated by his lack of autonomy in the court organization. He has no "service ideal"—which professional status implies—because his primary allegiance is to the organization rather than to his client.

That they are not regarded as professionals by their superiors is implicit in the probation officers' furtive complaint that judges frequently do not read their reports. Moreover, judges will often carefully select passages condemning the accused to be read aloud in the courtroom in justification of the sentence they have imposed. What supposedly is a confidential document is often cynically employed to validate judicial behavior or is otherwise used to reinforce administrative action already taken in connection with a plea or sentence. The fact that judges accept, reject, or modify the impact of pre-sentence probation reports destroys any sort of possible professional relationship between probation officers and the court organization or the client.

The circumstances under which probation reports are prepared cast serious doubts on their objectivity, validity, and integrity. The civil service, bureaucratic work situation, as it affects the possibility of impartially gathering "facts" about an accused, makes for the problematic and tenuous character of the enterprise. The Supreme Court's confidence in the pre-sentence investigation as an impartial means of gathering facts is hardly justified in light of the realities of the court organizations.

First, there is the matter of the case load. Authorities in the field suggest, for example, that twelve cases per month is the maximum any probation officer should be asked to handle adequately.[11] If he is performing supervision services as well, the maximum should be six. In Metropolitan Court eighteen to twenty cases per month are a common pre-sentence investigation case load.[12] In addition to various "short cuts" and work "crimes" which enable a probation officer to handle an otherwise impossible load, the use of clichés and stereotypes to characterize defendants helps to reduce the strain. That is to say, besides information from public and similar documents as to age, marital status, education, employment record, prior military history, prior medical history, and the like, the pre-sentence reports read remarkably alike. At the outset of his career in Metropolitan Court, each probation officer is carefully indoctrinated to emphasize only those aspects of a defendant's social biography and character which are consistent with his *new* status. Positive virtues are rarely stressed, if ever, except in passing. In order to assure that the reports submitted for judicial inspection contain the kind of negative material desired by the court administration, the probation supervisors must edit and rewrite, if necessary, in Orwellian fashion, material already submitted by a probation officer. Often the reports contain glib, unsupportable generalizations about an accused's character—at best explicable in terms of a striving for consistency. One of the leading Metropolitan Court lawyers sardonically refers to the probation staff as "the character assassins."

Frustrated as professionals, stripped of real decision-making power, lacking a genuine career motif, and assigned relatively low status by the community, it is not surprising that probation workers often develop a high degree of cynicism. They come to view their administrators as frightened, insecure, petty officials who will respond to any organizational need at the expense of workers and clients. There is a constant undercurrent of antagonism between probation workers and their supervisors. Possessed of a middle-class pseudo-gentility, they are offended and intimidated by what they perceive to be ruthlessness and insensitivity on the part of their administrators. Similarly, they are also constantly appalled by their clients' crimes and the seemingly general misconduct of their private lives.

As a consequence, in order to avoid being deceived or manipulated by administrators or clients, probation workers adopt an intellectual stance of misanthropy. It is translated into their pre-sentence reports, which reflect these harsh attitudes of displaced hostility. Thus, while their negative evaluation of offenders is in part organizationally induced, it is also a result of the attitudes they have developed in response to tensions and pressures in their work lives.

There is, however, still another aspect to the matter: the drabness and monotony of probation work are relieved to some extent by the defendants themselves. They who have often violated the middle-class ethic of restraint point up to the probation officers the prosaic, lackluster character of their own lives. Both probation and psychiatry afford unique opportunities for what may be called "occupational voyeurism." The practitioners have an unusual work situation in which they can practice self-titillation by vicariously experiencing the life-style of the "other." The possibilities of unrestrained voyeurism are an unanticipated job bonus. There is a good deal of covert thrill-seeking for the probation officer or psychiatrist as he elicits details of an accused's prior social-emotional experience. Often it furnishes a stark, heady contrast to the conventional and pedestrian style of life of the minor civil servant. To affirm the superiority and validity of his own middle-class existence, it follows that the defendant and the life-style which brought him to the criminal court must be negatively construed and reported by the probation officer or psychiatrist.

The attempt to alleviate tedium manifests itself in still another way. Consigned to rigid salary schedules and job duties, the probation worker tries to find some status distinctions in his homogeneous occupational mass. So he invents synthetic, or at least contrived, ranks according to skill and expertise, as well as seniority. Thus in the Metropolitan Court probation division there is a twofold distinction in office location—"wall" men and "cubicle" men. Wall men merit an office along the walls of the court building, one with windows. These workers usually receive the more "important" cases in terms of complexity or notoriety, or the case of a public figure.

Probation administrators view the assignment of an "important" case as prestigious for the worker. Actually it presents him with additional pressures because the case is well above the routine. Old hands, in time, treat the "celebrity's" case with the same perfunctoriness they treat other cases. This is the only way they can deal effectively with a crushing work load further complicated by the "important" case.

With the "celebrity" or "very important person," however,

there is opportunity for a special kind of casework voyeurism. The probation worker has an officially supported opportunity to observe intimately unfamiliar life-styles, and to interact with persons he might never know otherwise. These brief excursions into the homes and offices of those who may possess power, influence, and wealth heighten the civil servant's feelings of profound inadequacy. Cynicism and misanthropy, as emotional shield and character armor, are reinforced and strengthened.

"Cubicle" men occupy small, windowless offices and are assigned the most routine, perfunctory cases. Generally, these are the large majority of case situations in which, very simply, a report is needed in the files to "cover" the case. Much of the pre-sentence probation effort is of this nature—voluminous files of appropriate letters, forms, and a report (including several carbon copies) replete with clichés and appropriate stereotypes, all serving to rationalize and codify the basis for disposition or sentence. These are pointed to with pride as the justification for the organization's existence and as the implementation of its goals to "individualize" justice. There are sporadic occasions, especially in connection with the case of a "celebrity," when all the resources and skills of the court's auxiliary services are invoked. When this happens, an incredibly intensive, systematic, rigorous, and precise job of evaluation is often the result. But even then, the material is used selectively rather than "scientifically."

In the main, the importance of the pre-sentence investigation as a decision-making tool for the judge is overrated. It is helpful in those situations where there are no other criteria available, such as in the case of a minor first offender, or where the offense is a minor one and the complainant is not an influential individual. But in the case of a defendant with a long criminal history, his "record" will be the most important basis for decision-making, rather than the investigation. And when politically visible criteria enter the picture, the pre-sentence report is virtually ignored. Judges generally discount the reports because of what they consider a major legal flaw—their hearsay nature. Meanwhile, probation workers are busily copying out each other's files, quoting verbatim from the often unverified, speculative, hearsay material about an accused or his family and relatives. This mass of data is then sifted and tailored to fit some preconceived model of the offender. The truly incredible aspect of the whole matter is that the pre-sentence report and the questionable information on which it may be based follow a convicted individual to wherever he may be committed and are further used as a basis for classification at the institution.

The really significant function of a probation division in the criminal court—that of "cooling out" an accused who has pleaded to a lesser offense—is barely recognized. When an accused has reached that stage in his career where he has pleaded, he is ready "to tell his side of the story." The probation officer is the ideal vehicle for this catharsis; he is a "helping" person who will communicate with the judge for the accused. But a more realistic appraisal of the social situation is expressed by Robert K. Merton in another context when he talks about the basis for reciprocal mistrust in our society:

> In place of a sense of Gemeinschaft—a genuine community of values—there intrudes pseudo-Gemeinschaft—the feigning of personal concern with the other fellow in order to manipulate him the better.[13]

The pseudo-Gemeinschaft used by a probation officer or psychiatrist is part of an effort to obtain information for his report—"to get the client to open up"—and also serves as a means of "cooling out" the defendant. For in most instances an accused will see his interview with the probation officer and psychiatrist as possibly helpful to his cause, unmindful of his being manipulated for organizational ends.

THE JARGON OF DISPARAGEMENT

In view of the content of most pre-sentence investigation reports, there has been a good deal of debate about whether their contents should be made available to an accused for a chance to cross-examine or contradict. Social agencies and similar organizations, including law enforcement agencies, object to relaxing restrictions on the confidentiality of the reports. They insist that secrecy be maintained on the usual bureaucratic grounds that the sources of information would be loath to furnish data, and agencies would be unwilling to exchange information with each other, if the nature and sources of the information were revealed. The fact remains that the reports are usually interlarded with vituperative and pre-judicial epithets of the most loose, inaccurate, and vague diagnostic meaning. Frequently employed are such terms as "immoral," "depraved," "corrupt," "psychopathic," "immature," "weak-willed," "inadequate," "unconventional," "egocentric-aggressive individual," "primitive," "suggestible," "anti-social," "sexual deviate," "emotionally unstable," "shiftless," and "immature and maladjusted." In place of hard data and precise formulation, these labels often form the basis of an administrative decision involving a person's liberty or confinement. The civil service malaise substitutes administrative mediocrity of thought and performance because it is cheaper, quicker, and more productive of statistically visible results in support of the organizational budget request.

During 1964 the Metropolitan Court psychiatric clinic examined 2,213 people for the court. Of these, only eighty-one were found to be suffering from a clinically identifiable psychosis, and nine from a psychoneurosis. The remainder were assigned ad hoc labels of diagnostic convenience—with or without addiction to drugs or alcohol. Others were assigned "lesser character disorders," including various forms of "emotional instability," "aggressive reaction," or "aggressive and anti-social reaction." Other psychiatric diagnoses employed most frequently were: "Aggression Released by Alcohol," "Immature Adult," "Immature Maladjusted Adolescent," "Inadequate—with Drug Addiction," "Dull Adynamic," "Adjusted to Low Cultural Level," and "Pathologic-Emotionally Unstable."

These labels were incorporated in the pre-sentence probation reports, which in addition contain their own evaluations. The following are exact reproductions of several reports:

"K" is of average height, sturdy build and brown complexion. He wears glasses and is neat in regard to his dress and personal appearance.

Exceedingly polite, friendly, congenial and at times ingratiating, the defendant was normally rather nervous during interviews. Obviously attempting to present himself most favorably, he frequently expressed apprehension concerning the outcome of his predicament. Vague and evasive in regard to his discussion of the offense, despite his eventual admissions, he impressed as being shrewd, calculating, unethical and not too reliable an informant. Basically inadequate, his narcissism and egocentricity are readily apparent.

The defendant was reared primarily in this city by his parents in modest economic circumstances. He was apparently well behaved as a child and provided with sound religious and moral training. But apparently for economic reasons, he never completed high school. Nothing is now presently known of his early aspirations; however, it appears he has for several years been interested in medicine, or allied fields, which he was often not qualified to pursue because of the lack of at least an academic high school diploma.

He has for several years worked as a masseur and more recently as a chiropractor, unquestionably enjoying the prestige attached to the erroneous title many have bestowed upon him, namely that of "Dr. K."

He entered a succession of marriages, virtually nothing being known directly of the earliest, and he now admits to fathering at least three out-of-wedlock children. While he has undoubtedly supported his homes properly, in recent years he has provided little companionship to his present wife, who he unquestionably dominates. His marital adjustments were adversely affected by his egocentricity.

"J" is a physically well-developed and light-complexioned individual, who wears eyeglasses, is neat and clean in his personal appearance and is well spoken as an interview subject.

Of apparently average intelligence, the product of a broken home, in which he was in contact with rejecting, inadequate, disinterested and seemingly immoral parental figures, the defendant, throughout his formative years, led an unstable existence devoid of parental affection or guidance or emotional or economic security. Deprived of a normal home life, he accordingly appears to have developed at an early age an attitude of rebellion and resentment towards his relatives and authority and to have found expression in the commission of overt acts.

Basically he is an overly aggressive, immature, emotionally unstable individual, who is seemingly by nature weak willed and suggestible, lacks adequate ethical or moral standards and seeks release of latent feelings of hostility towards his mother by armed assaults, predominantly upon women. Impulsive and unpredictable, he seemingly attempts to emulate the role of a mature and stable individual but when overwhelmed by feelings of inadequacy and the responsibilities attendant upon such a role, resorted to a previously indicated pattern of behavior. Agency reports, however, indicate that the defendant's neurological disorder alone cannot be made responsible for his anti-social activities.

"Y" is a tall, slim individual with a prominent scar on his forehead. His arms are also heavily scarred from the intravenous use of drugs. In the interview situation, he related in a shallow, apathetic and dull manner. Notwithstanding, he appears to be rather cunning, shrewd, unreliable and anti-social in his attitude.

The product of a broken home occasioned by the death of his father during his childhood, the defendant was haphazardly reared without the benefit of competent direction and supervision by his financially harassed mother. In his early adolescence, "Y" associated himself with a disorderly neighborhood group, whose behavior patterns he emulated and which culminated in his periodic drinking, sexual promiscuity and gambling while visiting commercialized establishments, in the vicinity of his work. He hence experienced successive appearances in the Children's Court and was twice committed to the State Training School for Boys. Institutionalization and supervision at that time failed to positively modify his behavior and attitudes and he has followed a similar pattern during his adulthood.

During at least the past three years, by his own admission, he has been addicted to the use of heroin and seemingly, fundamentally weak-willed and inadequate, it is apparent he has lacked any significant inclination to discontinue using narcotics following releases from confinement. On the contrary, he has continued to closely associate with undesirable persons of both sexes, including some of his relatives who are also drug addicts. His early home environment including his wife's record and her drug addiction have manifestly significantly contributed to his continued delinquencies and in general, he has lived in surroundings where he has been exposed to pernicious influences and temptations to which he eventually succumbed.

Irregularly employed, it seems apparent he had at least, recently, resorted to selling narcotics in addition to other illegal activities to support his own habit and for his own individual profit.

The defendant is a plump individual of average height who presents a good appearance. When interviewed, she was calm, poised and unabashedly forthright and frank in discussing the instant offense and her personal affairs.

As a result of the influence of her parents, especially her mother, the defendant appears at an early age to have become materialistically oriented. Simultaneously she also seems to have acquired strong needs to dominate in compensation for the domination to which she was subjected. Her father's ineffectuality in relationship to her mother appears to have imbued her with a lack of respect for male figures and a concept of the male as a sub-missive figure. Her married life appears to have strengthened and intensified that concept.

"X" is a capable, egocentric and aggressive individual whose moral and ethical sensibilities appear to be nonexistent, or at best, blunted. Her activities in recent years have been characterized by her hedonistic, self-centered, unconventional and calculatedly dishonest behavior. She has displayed no capacity for loyalty either to her husband or her employer. In relation to the instant offense, she displays no real feelings of remorse or penitence but rather appears to believe that by her forthright admissions and offers of restitution, she has completely relieved herself from all burden of guilt and will thus escape further punishment for her actions.

In upholding pre-sentence probation reports and their propriety within the meaning of due process, the Supreme Court has stated: "Probation workers making reports of their investigations have not been trained to prosecute but to aid offenders." [14] But in view of the actual nature of many pre-sentence reports, the Supreme Court's confidence is at best without a firm basis in reality. The reports expertly use the sweeping generalization to characterize the defendant—but adroitly hedged with an appropriate degree of tentativeness, to make an otherwise pejorative comment appear "objective."

The disclosure of pre-sentence reports would probably at least help to make the reports more circumspect and moderate in their assertions and characterizations. As matters now stand, the defend-ant's side of the story gets short shrift. For example, accounts of police brutality, which *do* occur, are almost never mentioned in the reports. Similarly, the likelihood that a complainant in the case may *also* have been involved as a guilty participant in the crime in question is never indicated. If the information is included, it is usually later deleted. Too often, in summary, what is sought is a balanced psychiatric-probation document which will be consonant with a defendant's new status.

To remedy this deficiency of the present system of criminal justice, it may be necessary at the very least to furnish psychiatric and probation services which will speak in behalf of the accused. This may seem like a preposterous suggestion, but the alternative —more resources and personnel at the disposal of the existing organization—would only reinforce the present functions of psychiatry and probation and further prevent a truly adversary system of criminal justice.

8

The convergence of the adversary and bureaucratic models

> "My object all sublime I shall achieve in time
> —to make the punishment fit the crime."
> —William S. Gilbert, *The Mikado*

Throughout this book we have been describing two systems or models of criminal justice. One is couched in constitutional-ideological terms of due process and rule of law; it is the one we think we have, or ought to have. The other model of criminal justice is the administrative, ministerial, rational-bureaucratic one we have actually institutionalized. It is also, perhaps, the system we really desire to maintain. While we continue to express our preference and reverence for the constitutional ideology, it is the perfunctory and efficacious system of justice that we implement. In large measure we do so because of its value and utility for each actor in the system.

Tensions and pressures within the criminal court, and criticisms of it by vested interest groups, are products of the inability to reconcile the two modes of justice and their conflicting ideologies. Failures, shortcomings, and oppressive features of our system of criminal justice have been blamed on a variety of sources, including "lawless" police, overzealous district attorneys, "hanging" juries, general corruption and political chicanery, incompetent judges, inadequate counsel, or the social disabilities of the defendant. But the ideological qualities of due process have served largely to conceal the drift toward the mediocrity of assembly-line justice.

The traditional rules of due process were designed to uniformly, fairly, and reasonably establish the guilt or innocence of an accused *regardless* of individual characteristics. The deflection of due process goals to those of efficiency and production has been aided and abetted by the emergence of "socialized" courts, which have furnished the means for achieving the new goals. "Individualization" in reality *depersonalizes* the individual and renders him more tractable and amenable to the organizational designs of the court. The apotheosis of the "socialized" court is the juvenile court, which made its first appearance in America in Chicago in 1899.

Unlike the adult criminal court where, at least in theory, the primary question is one of guilt or innocence *regardless* of particular qualities or characteristics of the accused, in the "socialized" court the line of inquiry is completely reversed. Determination of guilt or innocence in the form of "Did he or didn't he?" becomes secondary. The paramount questions concern the character and background of the accused, his needs and problems—questions which in traditional due process were not supposed to be raised, at least until guilt had been determined. The philosophy of the juvenile court is predicated on the notion that the court acts like a parent: it does not "punish" but tries to understand, correct, and help children who have run afoul of the law. The child is not a "criminal" but rather a ward of the state. Thus the adversary presumption of the adult criminal court is replaced by probation and psychiatric reports and the testimony of social workers and other interested experts, all of whom attempt to clarify the child's "problem" so that he may be "treated." Guilt or innocence is relatively unimportant, and the procedures are entirely informal.

Because of the "non-criminal" nature of the court, it was thought that "socialized" courts need not conform to the usual constitutional guarantees required in the case of a person actually charged with a crime. Such tortuous logic has brought a flood of serious criticism. Paul Tappan charges that the state, under the guise of protecting a child, tends "to rationalize the abandonment, partial or complete, of even the most basic conceptions of due process of law: a specific charge; confrontation by one's adverse witnesses; right to counsel and appeal; rejection of prejudicial, irrelevant, and hearsay testimony; adjudication only upon proof . . ." [1]

The standards employed in the respective courts are decidedly dissimilar. In juvenile court a child is "adjudicated" on the basis of a "fair preponderance of the evidence," which is a significantly easier criterion for organizational personnel than the evidence "beyond a reasonable doubt" required in an adult criminal court. And it is of course a fiction that a child who is adjudged "delinquent" in the course of a "socialized" process is not a "criminal" and does not have a "record." True, he does not in the adult sense of the word, but as a sharply practical matter and for purposes of future employment, military service, and other similar situations, he does. This harsh reality has recently caused the philosophy and the constitutional propriety of the juvenile court to be reviewed.[2] As a result, most of the constitutional rules and procedural requirements of the adult criminal court have been made relevant in the organizational structure of the juvenile court, just as the ameliorative-therapeutic features of the juvenile court have become an important aspect of the adult criminal court. But when the process of convergence is complete, both courts will have become even more rational, their bureaucratic instruments even stronger and more elaborate. Their "success" in their respective spheres will be near perfect in terms of the total number of "adjudications" and "convictions."

The emergence of the "socialized" techniques of the juvenile court, in other words, has furnished the adult criminal court with further means for attaining deflected goals. The new goals of rationality have precluded the sort of individualization required by the traditions of due process. Instead, the ameliorative-therapeutic techniques of the "socialized" courts have been appropriated for the purpose of "individualizing" defendants and accused persons. The individualizing which takes place, however, while it may conceivably help an accused in terms of sentence or disposition, is used mainly to further organizational ends of affixing guilt. The great investment of effort, resources, and personnel does not implement constitutional due process presumptions of innocence in behalf of the accused. On the contrary, the tacit assumption of the criminal court system is, "Where there's smoke, there's fire!"

The "youthful offender" is the paradigmatic illustration of the convergence of traditional legalism and the "socialized" features of the juvenile court. Elements of both systems are drawn together to furnish the most rational and efficient world for both the organization and the accused. Each offender is individualized. The formal legalism of the traditional adult criminal court is appropriated for the most part, but the additional dimensions of pretrial psychiatric examination and probation investigation are invoked for structural reinforcement. This special procedure is offered by the criminal court to a young adult over sixteen but not yet nineteen, who is charged with a crime. The alleged advantages are virtually equivalent to those of his younger contemporary in the juvenile court. The proceedings are confidential; the records are "sealed" and secret; the young person will not have a criminal record because the original "criminal" charges are dropped in favor of the appellation of "youthful offender." Even some of the juvenile court's semantics are adopted to minimize the criminal image of the procedure. Thus, for example, an offender is not indicted; instead a "bill" or "complaint" is drawn against him. The youth is not convicted; he is "adjudicated" a youthful offender. The bare bones of the traditional legal requirements of the adult criminal court are otherwise maintained—there is a right to a trial, but by a judge sitting without jury; there is a right to counsel (unlike the case formerly in many juvenile courts); and the rules of evidence are observed. But presumption of innocence is seriously eroded from the outset, because youthful offender treatment is considered a "privilege" for a young person charged with a crime. He must apply for such status and must consent in advance to waive any constitutional privilege against self-incrimination by submitting to a detailed social, psychological, and psychiatric investigation. If he qualifies on the basis of this inquiry (or what amounts to extensive "mindtapping," to use Szasz's term), he will be tried as a youthful offender rather than for a specific crime.

The criteria used to determine a youth's suitability for "treatment" are primarily those elements in his past conduct, his present psychological state, and his social history which would indicate that he could adapt to society in the future. It must be noted again that this comprehensive procedure is employed before any determination of guilt or innocence. The cooperation of the accused is almost a foregone conclusion, for the bait dangled before him is that should he be found guilty he will at worst be designated a youthful offender. *But* the youth is first required to demonstrate effectively his "cooperative" attitude by indicating his guilt during his probation investigation! Failure to affirm his guilt beforehand impairs his eligibility for youthful offender treatment.

As in the case of the adult criminal, the lawyer plays a critical role as agent-mediator for the youthful offender. But in this instance he has a good deal more to offer an accused and his kin group in the way of tangible benefits, in return for their cooperation. For a young person accused of a serious crime, the possibility of receiving youthful offender treatment can be much more acceptable than possible conviction of even a misdemeanor. There is no hesitation whatsoever if the original charge is a felony. The thought of "social treatment," confidential proceedings, and the "no criminal record" features of the procedure are an irresistible lure, stimulating the family's eager cooperation. They do not consider that for all practical purposes the youth will have a criminal record, nor do they know that the "socialized" youthful offender procedure produces virtually a 100 per cent conviction rate.

Table 9 shows the disposition of all "youth" cases processed during 1963 in Metropolitan Court. Of 419 accused who were initially arraigned in the Youth section of the court, 154 were disapproved for possible youthful offender treatment as a result of preliminary investigation, and their disposition can be compared in Table 10 (page 176). These individuals were then processed through the regular adult criminal court of Metropolitan Court. Of those 260 who were "approved" for possible treatment as youthful offenders, only three were actually acquitted after trial. Only one other youth was discharged on his own recognizance, after trial.

Table 9: Dispositions of "youth" cases in Metropolitan Court (1963)

Total youth arraigned	419	
Approved for possible "YO" treatment	260	
Disapproved after investigation	154	
Transferred to other courts as underage	5	

Youthful offender dispositions (260)		Per cent of total
Sentence suspended—probation	148	56.9
Sentence suspended—no probation	3	1.2
Committed to institutions	68	26.2
Alpha Reception Center	47	
Beta Reformatory	17	
Sigma State Farm	4	
Sentence to time already served	6	2.3
Tried and acquitted	3	1.2
Discharged after trial	1	.4
Sentence deferred (restitution)	4	1.5
Cases pending	27	10.4
TOTAL	260	100.1% *

* Rounded to nearest tenth of a per cent.

Thus the remarkably slim possibility of avoiding conviction in the regular adult procedure in Metropolitan Court, as may be seen in Tables 1 and 3, is narrowed even further when the bare bones of traditional legalism are fused with the socialized features of the ameliorative-therapeutic model in the youthful offender proceeding.

Table 10 shows the eventual disposition of youths who were disapproved for youthful offender treatment and thereafter processed like any adult criminal in Metropolitan Court. That is to say, *almost* like any adult criminal, for there is now an important difference. A complete psychological, psychiatric, and social dossier, including a probation report, is now available to the prosecuting authority, and what began as an unequal contest becomes a foregone conclusion of defeat for these defendants. They had gambled on the possibility of receiving youthful offender treatment, and in the process they had furnished a welter of self-incriminatory data which they might not otherwise have done. Note that of the 154 disapproved youths, only one was acquitted and only one other was dismissed after an indictment had been filed against him. Of the total group of disapproved youths, eighty-five were white males and sixty-six Negro males. There were also three females, two white and one Negro. The group is quite similar in socio-demographic characteristics to the regular adult criminal population in Metropolitan Court, except for age. But the age factor, which is ordinarily mitigating, did not help this group at all.

Overall, these disapproved youths not only fared more poorly than the youthful offenders, but they were dealt with more severely than their adult contemporaries in the regular criminal court process of Metropolitan Court. Approximately 13 per cent of the disapproved group received a probation disposition, compared with 57 per cent of the adjudged YO group and 30 per cent of the overall adult criminal cases (including the disapproved youths) during the same year.

Authorities have long emphasized the need to liberalize the bail system in order to help the accused develop his defense; but the

Table 10: Disposition of disapproved youths in Metropolitan Court (1963)

		Per cent of disapproved cases
Sentenced to prison after pleading	95	61.7
Placed on probation	21	13.6
Other sentences or dispositions	38	24.7
Sentence suspended, released to warrant on another charge	1	2.6
Committed to State Hospital	1	2.6
Pending cases	30	78.9
Sentence deferred, to make restitution	2	5.3
Tried and acquitted	1	2.6
Indictment dismissed	1	2.6
Sentence suspended, no probation	2	5.3
	(38)	(99.9) *
TOTAL	154	100.0

* Rounded to nearest tenth of a per cent.

youthful offender process deflates this notion as well. Approximately two-thirds of the 260 youthful offenders were on bail status or paroled in the custody of their attorneys or parents at the time of their adjudication; the remainder were "jail" cases, not admitted to bail or parole (see Table 11). But jail-bail status did not

Table 11: Status of approved youthful offenders at time of adjudication (1963)

		Per cent of total
Released on bail	179	68.85
Paroled	16	6.15
Prison	65	25.00
TOTAL	260	100.00

materially affect the eventual outcome—a nearly 100 per cent conviction rate. The "socialized" court procedure and other organizational elements seemingly canceled out any advantages that may have accrued in connection with bail or parole status.

While the pre-pleading investigation is uniformly employed in the case of the youthful offender, it is increasingly used with adult accused persons in Metropolitan Court and elsewhere, especially when vital information is sought by the court and prosecution to complete their case. Because the accused must waive some of his rights, there is a tacit element of quid pro quo involved. The accused is led to believe he will be administratively rewarded, in terms of plea and sentence, beyond the degree that the usual justice by negotiation and bargaining may have availed. Again, the traditional adversary model of due process is virtually ignored; the procedures are administrative, clinical, bureaucratic. The effort at individualization is not in terms of ideal notions of due process but is directed toward meeting the needs of the organization.

More important, in the convergence model the individual accused is himself drawn into and made an integral part of the system. Under the guise of individualization, the accused becomes an active, vital element in his own processing. In an important sense, then, the convergence model of the criminal court is the most rational evolution of that institution, for it effectively diminishes or minimizes individual motives and concerns. In short, the individual is reduced virtually to a cipher. Criminal court organizations become all apparatus and instrumentality—with no socially viable end in view other than their production figures.

JUSTICE BY NEGOTIATION

Amitai Etzioni has distinguished between "survival" and "effectiveness" models of organization:

> A system model constitutes a statement about relationships which, if actually existing, would allow an organization to main-

tain itself and to operate. There are two major sub-types of system models. One may be called a survival model—i.e., a set of requirements which, if fulfilled, allows the system to exist. In such a model, each relationship specified is a prerequisite for the functioning of the system; remove any one of them and the system ceases to operate, like an engine whose sparkplugs have been removed. The second sub-type is an effectiveness model. It defines a pattern of interrelations among the elements of the system which would make it most effective in the service of a given goal, as compared to other combinations of the same or similar elements. The question here is: Which type of sparkplug makes the engine run smoothest? [3]

But we cannot analyze the organization of the criminal court without referring to its goals. If we were to base our analysis on the court's objectives of "due process" and "justice," then the organization quite simply has not survived. At least it has ceased to exist in terms of those organizational objectives and goals. But in terms of an "effectiveness" model, and as an institutional arrangement, the criminal court has been eminently "successful" in that it is most "effective." While its effectiveness is not related to the traditional goals of the criminal court, the court is highly efficient and rational in terms of those goals as they have been displaced or deflected.

Our purpose has been to try to understand, and to distinguish between, the system of criminal justice men believe they have or ought to have, and the institutional activity that really exists. One must first identify the system and its dimensions before considering alternatives. The question then becomes, "Which values shall men pursue?" If men have internalized values which reward rational conduct and maximum production, then those values will be controlling. They will serve as the benchmark in all human activity, including the administration of justice.

Science remains incapable of furnishing the answers to the "ought"—what ought men to do?—or what values men must believe in or obey, or the validity of those values. But given the values men do possess, social science can furnish knowledge about the system of justice by negotiation which has developed in pursuit of those values. The system is a response to social and organizational pressures, and it meets the real needs of everyone involved in the system. These may include the urgent need of the warden to keep the jail population flowing; the judge to clear his calendar; the district attorney to maximize his "batting average"; the lawyer to enhance his stock-in-trade as an influential agent who is all things to all men; the police to expedite their cases and utilize the pressures of bargaining to get information for their activities; and certainly for the accused to benefit from a lesser plea and a more lenient disposition which would not otherwise be available.

But apart from questions of the legality of bargaining, there remain ethical and practical problems. Bargain-counter justice is like the proverbial iceberg: much of the system's potential danger is hidden by secret negotiations, and its least alarming feature, the final plea, is the one presented to public view. Secrecy creates possibilities and opportunities fraught with the danger of venal and dishonest release of defendants on the pretext of "bargaining." And there is the distinct possibility that dangerous individuals may receive inadequate punishment because of the bargaining system. Conversely, the gullible, unsophisticated defendant, who may be innocent, can be victimized through the manipulation of organizational pressures. Regardless of the advantages or hazards of bargaining, the system is fortified and sustained by the vested interests of the court personnel and other participants. The organization is geared to production. It must deal with large numbers of cases and at the same time attempt a delicate balance of competing interests.

SOME IMPLICATIONS FOR THE FUTURE

The institutional position of the criminal court may be analogous to the following description of the traffic problem in New York City:

> Up and down the blocks off Seventh Avenue between Thirty-Fifth and Fortieth Streets, parking is forbidden, but trucks line every foot of curb. One even occupies the restricted zone in front of a firehouse. Without such wholesale violation of parking regulations, the city's garment industry could not survive. Even so, the number of workers in the needle trades has steadily dwindled, partly because small employers cannot bear the cost of fighting city traffic. So completely has the formal system of traffic control broken down in the garment district that only the illegal and tenuously viable one is upheld. On Thirty-Sixth Street a policeman, his shirt stained black from perspiration, extricates a truck from the tangle of the street and guides the driver as he backs into an illegal parking space.[4]

Men must choose what they want. Shall it be rational values as they manifest themselves in maximum production and technically efficient allocation of resources, or shall it be the individual as an end in himself? For, as an idea, due process of law is incompatible with the inevitable idiosyncratic, deviant drives that are inherent in bureaucratic organization. That which C. Wright Mills called the "system of organized irresponsibility" cannot be simply attributed to the men involved. As Andrew Hacker indicates in discussing corporate and other large-scale organizations:

> . . . it does not matter who the officeholders are as individuals; for anyone placed in such an office would have much the same outlook and display much the same behavior . . . What is being said is that these institutions have lives and purposes of their own . . . If the man on the top sits at the controls, the car rides on rails he cannot move . . . our institutions are too large for a single individual to impress with his personality.[5]

Bureaucracy's thrust toward efficiency and power creates an administrative framework in the criminal court, and it functions independently to vitiate the idea of a combative, adversary system of justice. The seeming separateness of the parties (police, prosecution, judge, probation officer, psychiatrist, defense counsel, and accused) is illusory. On the contrary, these "adversaries" are integrated into a bureaucratic matrix. They are a functional system, eliminating any "separateness" that may have existed. The very fact that the parties are not independent helps to weaken the idea of truth through combat.

A theory of bureaucratization alone might be adequate to explain the weakening of the traditional concepts of justice and due process. But because the criminal court has also become an agency of rehabilitation, apart from its function of determining the truth, it is compromised as a judicial truth-seeking agency. In other words, the incorporation of ameliorative-therapeutic values and instruments into the court structure may maximize the court's effectiveness, but it negates the adversary idea of justice. Under the guise of psychological and social services, an accused and his family, together with the police, prosecution, judge, and probation personnel, enter into an arrangement wherein the court itself does no more than publicly affirm the informal arrangements that have been arrived at in camera.

One might argue that the adversary system is obsolete anyway, and that criminal courts can operate more efficiently and at less cost per case without the old-fashioned, clumsy, troublesome methods of due process. And, after all, doesn't "science" modernize justice, making it more speedy at least, and perhaps more precise? Perhaps so, but no known "scientific" procedures have demonstrated in rigorous empirical terms that they can *in fact* more readily sort out the innocent from the guilty than the adversary-combative system of due process.

The adversary system has always been an ideal goal at best. But its further erosion has been part of the larger institutional blight characterized by our "failure to invest in people." The United

States Supreme Court proposes, but the bargain system of criminal justice disposes. The most libertarian system of rules can be quite meaningless unless we have the resources to implement them and make them viable. Disneyland equivalents of bread and circuses, meaningless busywork in accumulating unusable military power drains our limited resources and produces not only a second-rate educational system and inadequate medical services but a shoddy system of criminal justice. The precarious state of the system can best be underscored by the fact that it would be paralyzed if every defendant asked for and received a jury trial. One federal judge recently indicated that "it would be 'anarchy' if every draft evader demanded and received a jury trial . . ." [6] It has been suggested that political and other dissidents could effectively paralyze our judicial institutions by engaging in widespread disorders for which large numbers would then invoke rights to a jury trial.

Since the system of justice by negotiation without trial is likely to continue to be the major feature of criminal justice for the foreseeable future, some suggestions for supervising the process would appear to be in order. It would not require great additional resources to charge some independent body, not enmeshed in the organizational framework of our court systems, to oversee and review guilty pleas. This person or group might resemble the office of the Swedish ombudsman or some version of the "Inspector-General." It would be wholly independent of the closed community of the criminal court and would scrupulously supervise each guilty plea to determine whether minimum standards had been met along the following lines of inquiry: [7]

(1) Was the indictment read and were the charges clearly explained to the defendant?

(2) If a defendant indicates that he desires to plead guilty, probe him as to the reasons for his desire to do so, and

(3) Explain to him the right of a jury trial.

(4) Ask the prosecution to summarize in detail the evidence *other than any confession* that has been obtained against the defendant.

(5) Examine carefully the precise circumstances of a defend-

ant's arrest and all police practices and activities that preceded and followed the arrest.

(6) Scrutinize each lesser plea transaction to determine whether any secret arrangements have been made under the threat or promise of some benefit that would or would not accrue to the accused, should he agree or fail to comply.

(7) Assess the health, age, education, race, and other factors, such as intelligence, which might affect a defendant's tractability and capacity to resist manipulation.

(8) Evaluate the effects of any period of confinement prior to pleading, its duration, and the living conditions during such detention.

While it is true that judges, police, prosecutors, defense lawyers, probation personnel, and others are now required to make some or all of these inquiries and assessments, they cannot be relied upon to do so in many routine cases. And, of course, all the various participants are so elaborately entangled with one another in occupational and organizational terms that their objectivity and evaluations are compromised by other goals they seek.

Despite the recent furor over the value and legality of confessions, the process of criminal law enforcement has always depended and will continue to depend on negotiated "bargain plea" confessions in open court (i.e., pleas of guilty), rather than on confessions wrung from an accused in the back room of a police station. The decisions of the Supreme Court directing states and localities to furnish counsel for indigent persons, and similar decisions enforcing due process requirements, have been regarded in legal circles as a most important development in American jurisprudence. But the limited data we have seen suggest that results in the future, at least at the felony level, will not be significantly different from those which now obtain.

In fact, the Supreme Court, in seeking to protect the rights of a defendant in a criminal case, has in these decisions failed to take into account three crucial aspects of life in the courts which may render the more liberal rules ineffectual:

(1) The informal structure of the court which seeks goals other

than those envisioned by the formal, traditional criteria of due process.

(2) The real nature of the relationship among lawyers and other professionals within the court organization.

(3) The actual dimensions of the lawyer-client relationship in the criminal court—as opposed to glamorous and heroic poses in movies, television, novels, and the press.

Together, the organizational, occupational, and structural features of the criminal court are formidable. They promote a rational, efficient system of maximum production which will not be easily overcome by additional counsel and similar resources, for they may in turn be absorbed by the organizational structure. The organizational network of the criminal court today stands interposed between the most libertarian rules and the accused person. The rules as enunciated by the Supreme Court are based on the supposed existence of an adversary model of criminal justice, but the adversary ideal is no more. The additional resources and personnel necessary to implement the traditional rules of due process will instead strengthen the *present* system of criminal justice. The bureaucracy will become even more efficient in the production of guilt.

Notes

CHAPTER 1: THE CRIMINAL COURT AS A SOCIAL PROBLEM

1. *New York Times,* March 10, 1965.
2. *Ibid.,* November 4, 1965.
3. *Ibid.,* February 5, 1966.
4. Herbert L. Packer, "Two Models of the Criminal Process," *University of Pennsylvania Law Review,* CXIII, No. 1 (November 1964), 1–68.
5. Yale Kamisar, Fred E. Inbau, and Thurman Arnold, *Criminal Justice in Our Time,* Charlottesville, Va., 1965, p. 20.
6. Herbert A. Bloch and Gilbert Geis, *Man, Crime, and Society,* New York, 1962, pp. 37–38.
7. Arnold S. Trebach, *The Rationing of Justice,* New Brunswick, N. J., 1964, p. 15.
8. Federal Bureau of Investigation, U.S. Department of Justice, *Uniform Crime Reports for the United States, 1964,* Washington, 1965, p. 108.
9. Ronald Goldfarb, *Ransom: A Critique of the American Bail System,* New York, 1965, p. 96.
10.

YEAR	1960	1961	1962	1963	1964	1965
Total number of defendants (cases term.)	29,864	29,881	30,013	31,546	31,437	32,078

Source: *Annual Report of the Director of the Administrative Office of the United States Courts,* Washington, 1965.

11. Lee Silverstein, *Defense of the Poor in Criminal Cases in American State Courts,* Chicago, 1965, I, 7.
12. *Ibid.,* p. 10.
13. U.S. Department of Health, Education and Welfare, Children's Buɾɛaɹ, Washington, D.C., *Juvenile Court Statistics—1964,* pp. 1–6.
14. The American Bar Foundation has recently completed a $520,000 study of the American system of criminal justice dealing with police, prosecution, the guilty plea, and sentencing. To date, two of the five projected volumes to come out of the study have been published: Wayne R. LaFave, *Arrest: The Decision to Take a Suspect into Custody,* Boston, 1965, and Donald J. Newman, *Conviction: The Determination of Guilt or Innocence Without Trial,* Boston, 1966. In large measure, however, their analyses proceed largely along familiar, legalistic lines of inquiry. Although painstaking in their detailing of the legal and admnistrative issues, they are notably lacking in any sort of systematic examination of the social structure of the system of criminal justice.

CHAPTER 2: THE TWILIGHT OF THE ADVERSARY SYSTEM

1. *Barron vs. Baltimore,* 7 Pet. 243 (1833).
2. For an exhaustive analysis of the issue, see Charles Fairman and Stanley Morrison, "Does the Fourteenth Amendment Incorporate the Bill of Rights? The Original Understanding," *Stanford Law Review,* II (December 1949), 5–139. Although Justice Black, in his appendix to *Adamson vs. California,* 332 U.S. 46 (1947), tries to make a case for the intention of the framers of the Fourteenth Amendment to incorporate the Bill of Rights against the states, the weight of historical evidence would appear to be to the contrary.
3. For the view that it is the task of Congress to provide a set of uniform criminal procedures for the states, see Donald C. Dowling, "Escobedo and Beyond: The Need for a Fourteenth Amendment Code of Criminal Procedure," *Journal of Criminal Law, Criminology and Police Science,* LVI, No. 2 (June 1965), 143–157.
4. See Claude R. Sowle, ed., *Police Power and Individual Freedom,* Chicago, 1962, *passim,* for an excellent review of some of the sharp differences which have existed from time to time between federal and state procedural standards in criminal cases.
5. *Palko vs. Connecticut,* 302 U.S. 319, at 325 (1937).
6. *Adamson vs. California,* 332 U.S. 46, at 67 (1947).
7. Lewis Mayers, *The American Legal System,* New York, 1955, p. 99; H. L. A. Hart, *The Concept of Law,* New York, 1961, p. 154; David

Fellman, *The Defendant's Rights,* New York, 1958, pp. 4–5; Edmond Cahn, ed., *The Great Rights,* New York, 1963, pp. 43–63. For a general discussion of the concept see Morris D. Forkosch, "American Democracy and Procedural Due Process," *Brooklyn Law Review,* XXIV (1958), 176–195. See also Lon L. Fuller, *The Morality of Law,* New Haven, 1964, *passim.*

8. "But due process, unlike some legal rules, is not a technical conception with a fixed content unrelated to time, place, and circumstances. Expressing as it does in its ultimate analysis respect enforced by law for that feeling of just treatment which has been evolved through centuries of Anglo-American constitutional history and civilization, due process cannot be imprisoned within the treacherous limits of any formula. Representing a profound attitude of fairness between man and man, and more particularly between the individual and government, 'due process' is compounded of history, reason, the past course of decisions . . . Due process is not a mechanical instrument. It is not a yardstick. It is a process. It is a delicate process of adjustment inescapably involving the exercise of judgment by those whom the constitution entrusted with the unfolding of the process." Justice Frankfurter, *Joint Anti-Fascist Refugee Committee vs. McGrath,* 341 U.S. 123 (1951), at 162–163.

9. See Paul A. Freund, *The Supreme Court of the United States,* Cleveland, 1961, pp. 45–49; and Arthur E. Sutherland, *Constitutionalism in America,* New York, 1965, pp. 530–533.

10. *Hurtado vs. California,* 110 U.S. 516, at 535 (1884).

11. *Brown vs. Board of Education of Topeka,* 347 U.S. 483 (1954).

12. *Rochin vs. California,* 342 U.S. 165 (1952).

13. *Breithaupt vs. Abram,* 352 U.S. 432 (1957).

14. *Schmerber vs. California,* 384 U.S. 757 (1966).

15. Volume 7, *Federal Register,* p. 1407 (1942).

16. *Hirabayashi vs. United States,* 320 U.S. 81 (1943). *Korematsu vs. United States,* 323 U.S. 214 (1944).

17. Edward S. Corwin, *The Constitution and What It Means Today,* New York, 1963, p. 68.

18. Carl Brent Swisher, *The Growth of Constitutional Power in the United States,* 2nd ed., Chicago, 1963, p. 179.

19. For a brief discussion of the manner in which the criminal law is utilized in totalitarian systems as a mechanism of social control, see Wolfgang Friedmann, *Law in a Changing Society,* Berkeley, 1959, p. 49. See also Nanette Dembitz, "Racial Discrimination and the Military Judgment: The Supreme Court's Korematsu and Endo Decisions," *Columbia Law Review,* XLV, No. 2 (March 1944), 175–239.

20. Justice Jackson underlined this proposition rather neatly in his vigorous dissent in *Korematsu vs. United States*, 323 U.S. 214 (1944), involving the order excluding the Japanese from the West Coast to relocation centers: "But once a judicial opinion rationalizes such an order to show that it conforms to the Constitution, or rather rationalizes the Constitution to show that the Constitution sanctions such an order, the Court for all time has validated the principle of racial discrimination in criminal procedure and of transplanting American citizens. The principle then lies about like a loaded weapon ready for the hand of any authority that can bring forward a plausible claim of urgent need. . . ."

21. Harold J. Berman, *Justice in the U.S.S.R.*, New York, 1963.

22. Raul Hilberg, *The Destruction of the European Jews*, Chicago, 1961. See also H. L. A. Hart, *The Concept of Law*, New York, 1961, *passim;* and Gideon Hausner, *Justice in Jerusalem*, New York, 1966.

23. See Arnold S. Trebach, *op. cit.*, Chapter 4.

24. An exhaustive but somewhat futile debate has been going on in sociology as to "who is the criminal?" Three basic responses have been forthcoming. The legalistic is, "Only those are criminals who have been adjudicated as such by the courts." Paul W. Tappan, "Who Is the Criminal?" *American Sociological Review*, XII (February 1947), 96–102. One sociological approach is that the designation of a person as a criminal by court procedures is not necessary for scientific purposes; all one must know is "that a certain class of acts is defined as crime and that a particular person has committed an act of this class." Edwin H. Sutherland and Donald R. Cressey, *Principles of Criminology*, 6th ed., Philadelphia, 1960, pp. 18–19. The other sociological approach is that "social groups create deviance by making the rules whose infraction constitutes deviance, and by applying those rules to particular people and labeling them as outsiders. . . . deviance is not a quality of the act the person commits, but rather a consequence of the application by others of rules and sanctions to 'offenders' . . . The deviant is one to whom that label has successfully been applied; deviant behavior is behavior people so label." Howard S. Becker, *Outsiders: Studies in the Sociology of Deviance*, New York, 1963, p. 9.

25. *McBoyle vs. United States*, 283 U.S. 25 (1931). See also *U.S. vs. Lattimore*, 215 F. 2nd 845 (1954). Lattimore was charged with perjury for denying under oath that he had been following "the communist party line"—charges against him were dismissed as vague and nebulous.

26. See Claude R. Sowle, ed., *op. cit.*, p. 164; *McNabb vs. United States*, 318 U.S. 332 (1943); *Mallory vs. United States*, 354 U.S. 449 (1957).

27. See, for example, Fred Inbau and John Reid, *Lie Detection and Criminal Interrogation*, 3rd ed., Baltimore, 1953, *passim*.

28. See Nathan R. Sobel, "The Exclusionary Rules in the Law of Confessions: A Legal Perspective—A Practical Perspective," *New York Law Journal*, November 15, 1965.

29. In *Malloy vs. Hogan*, 378 U.S. 1 (1964), the Fifth Amendment, indicating that "no person . . . shall be compelled in any criminal case to be a witness against himself . . .", was held to apply to the states by way of the Fourteenth Amendment.

30. *Mapp vs. Ohio*, 367 U.S. 643 (1961). This was the decision to which Senator Goldwater, during the 1964 campaign, frequently referred as being responsible for the increase in crime because it impeded law enforcement officers.

31. *Gideon vs. Wainwright*, 372 U.S. 335 (1963). For a popular account of this historic development, see Anthony Lewis, *Gideon's Trumpet*, New York, 1964. For a historical analysis of the right to counsel, see William M. Beaney, *The Right to Counsel in American Courts*, Ann Arbor, 1955. See also, Note, "Counsel at Interrogation," *Yale Law Journal*, LXXIII (May 1964), 1000–1057.

32. With the passage of the Criminal Justice Act of 1964, indigent accused persons in the federal courts will be defended by federally paid legal counsel. For a general discussion of the nature and extent of public and private legal aid in the United States, see Emery A. Brownell, *Legal Aid in the United States*, Rochester, N.Y., 1961. Also, Ronald Goldfarb, "Crime, Wealth and Justice," *New Republic*, August 22, 1964, pp. 15–16.

33. For a discussion of the minimum requisites of a federal jury trial see David Fellman, *op. cit.*, pp. 86–90. Apparently there are three basic elements: (1) at least twelve persons must be on the panel; (2) a supervising judge must have power to instruct and advise as to law and facts; (3) the verdict must be unanimous. State requirements tend to vary in their detailed procedures. In the case of lesser offenses (misdemeanors), states can apparently dispense with jury trials. But once there is a trial of any kind, it must constitute a "fair" and orderly trial.

34. In *Robinson vs. California*, 370 U.S. 660 (1962), the court ruled that the provisions of the Eighth Amendment were applicable to the states. The jailing of a defendant suffering from drug addiction was adjudged to violate the constitution in that it inflicted "cruel and unusual punishment."

35. Abraham S. Goldstein, *"The State and the Accused: Balance of Advantage in Criminal Procedure," op. cit.*, p. 1163.

36. Jerome H. Skolnick, *Justice Without Trial*, New York, 1966, p. 241.
37. Donald J. Newman, *Conviction: The Determination of Guilt or Innocence Without Trial*, Boston, 1966, p. 3.
38. Lee Silverstein, *Defense of the Poor*, Chicago, 1965, p. 90.
39. ". . . Under our system of justice the most elemental concepts of due process of law contemplate that an indictment be followed by a trial, in an orderly courtroom, presided over by a judge, open to the public, and protected by all the procedural safeguards of the law." *Massiah vs. United States*, 377 U.S. 201 (1964), at p. 204.
40. Max Lerner, *America as a Civilization*, New York, 1957, p. 433.
41. Justice Arthur Goldberg, "Equal Justice for the Poor, Too," *New York Times Magazine*, March 15, 1964, p. 24. See also a most recent volume in this vein, Arnold S. Trebach, *op. cit., passim; Report of The Attorney General's Committee on Poverty and the Administration of Federal Criminal Justice*, Washington, 1963.
42. The basic proposition asserted here is reiterated in its classic version in Franz Alexander and Hugo Staub, *The Criminal, the Judge and the Public: A Psychological Analysis*, revised ed., New York, 1962, and in Philip Q. Roche, *The Criminal Mind*, New York, 1958.
43. Frederick Wertham, "Psychoauthoritarianism and the Law," *University of Chicago Law Review*, XXII, at p. 338.
44. Thomas S. Szasz, *Law, Liberty and Psychiatry*, New York, 1963, pp. 161–165.
45. *Ibid.*, pp. 165–169.
46. Karl F. Schuessler and Donald R. Cressey, "Personality Characteristics of Criminals," *American Journal of Sociology*, LV (March 1950), 476–484; S. R. Hathaway and Elio D. Monachesi, *Analyzing and Predicting Delinquency with the MMPI*, Minneapolis, 1953; Arthur P. Volkman, "A Matched Group Personality Comparison of Delinquent and Nondelinquent Juveniles," *Social Problems*, VI (Winter 1959), 238–245. For example, Guttmacher and Weihofen assert: "The authors are completely out of sympathy with those who maintain that all criminals are sick people and should be treated as such." M. S. Guttmacher and Henry Weihofen, *Psychiatry and the Law*, New York, 1952, p. 87. See also the following critiques of the psychiatric position: Barbara Wooton, *Social Science and Social Pathology*, London, 1959; Michael Hakeem, "A Critique of the Psychiatric Approach to Crime and Correction," *Law and Contemporary Problems*, XXIII (Autumn 1958), 650–682.
47. David Matza, *Delinquency and Drift*, New York, 1964, Chapter 4; Francis A. Allen, "Criminal Justice, Legal Values and the Rehabilitative Ideal," *Journal of Criminal Law, Criminology and Police Science*,

L, No. 3 (September–October 1959), 226–232; Thomas S. Szasz, *op. cit., passim;* Lewis Diana, "The Rights of Juvenile Delinquents: An Appraisal of Juvenile Court Procedures," *Journal of Criminal Law, Criminology and Police Science,* XLVII, No. 5 (January–February 1957), 561–569; Luis Kutner, "The Illusion of Due Process in Commitment Proceedings," *Northwestern University Law Review,* XLVII, 383–399; see also Thomas Szasz, *Psychiatric Justice,* New York, 1965.
48. George Feifer, *Justice in Moscow,* New York, 1965, p. 86.

CHAPTER 3: THE CRIMINAL COURT AS ORGANIZATION AND COMMUNICATION SYSTEM

1. Howard S. Becker, *The Other Side: Perspectives on Deviance,* New York, 1964, pp. 11–12.
2. See Paul W. Tappan, *Crime, Justice and Correction,* New York, 1960, pp. 342–344; David Fellman, *op cit.,* p. 63; Ernst W. Puttkammer, *Administration of Criminal Law,* Chicago, 1963, pp. 190–193; Lewis Mayers, *The Machinery of Justice,* Englewood Cliffs, N.J., 1963, pp. 104–105.
3. H. H. Gerth and C. Wright Mills, *From Max Weber: Essays in Sociology,* New York, 1958, p. 211.
4. Amitai Etzioni, *Modern Organizations,* Englewood Cliffs, N.J., 1964, pp. 94–104.
5. Aaron V. Cicourel, *Method and Measurement in Sociology,* New York, 1964, pp. 36–37.
6. See Jerome H. Skolnick, *op. cit.,* pp. 142–155, 174–175; Richard C. Donnelly, "Police Authority and Practices," *The Annals* (January 1962), pp. 90–110; Joseph Goldstein, "Police Discretion Not to Invoke the Criminal Process: Low Visibility Decisions in the Administration of Criminal Justice," *Yale Law Journal,* LXIX (March 1960), pp. 543–594.
7. *Uniform Crime Reports*—1963, Table 8, p. 93; 1964, Table 8, p. 95; 1965, Table 8, p. 97.
8. Adapted from Donald R. Cressey, "Crime," in Robert K. Merton and Robert A. Nisbet, eds., *Contemporary Social Problems,* New York, 1961, p. 29. Cressey based his version of Figure 2 on Walter A. Lunden, "How to Beat the Rap," *American Journal of Correction,* XIX (May–June 1957), p. 13.
9. Source: Nathan R. Sobel, *Brooklyn Law Review,* XXX, No. 1 (December 1963), p. 13.
10. Hugo A. Bedau, ed., *The Death Penalty in America,* Chicago, 1964, pp. 15–16.
11. E. H. Sutherland and D. R. Cressey, *op. cit.,* pp. 385–386; Charles

Winick, "The Psychology of Juries," in Hans Toch, ed., *Legal and Criminal Psychology*, New York, 1961, pp. 96–120; Charles L. Newman, "Trial by Jury: An Outmoded Relic?", *Journal of Criminal Law, Criminology and Police Science*, XLVI, No. 4 (November–December 1955), pp. 512–518.

12. Clarence C. Ferguson, Jr., "Formulation of Enforcement Policy: An Anatomy of the Prosecutor's Discretion Prior to Accusation," *Rutgers Law Review*, II (Spring 1957), p. 507; Newman F. Baker, "The Prosecutor—Initiation of Prosecution," *Journal of Criminal Law, Criminology and Police Science*, XXIII (January–February 1933), pp. 770–796.

13. Everett C. Hughes, *Men and Their Work*, Glencoe, Ill., 1958, pp. 131–138.

14. Erving Goffman, *Asylums*, pp. 127–169. See also a most recent example of the use of the "career" concept by a sociologist whose basic focus is the tuberculosis patient, but who also employs it in an analysis of prisoners, airline pilots, and business executives. Julius A. Roth, *Timetables: Structuring the Passage of Time in Hospital Treatment and Other Careers*, New York, 1963.

15. *Ibid.*, p. 128.

16. *Ibid.*, p. 168.

17. Lloyd E. Ohlin and Frank J. Remington, "Sentencing Structure: Its Effects Upon Systems for the Administration of Criminal Justice," *Law and Contemporary Problems*, XXIII (Summer 1958), pp. 495–507.

18. Erving Goffman, "On Cooling the Mark Out: Some Aspects of Adaptation to Failure," in Arnold M. Rose, ed., *Human Behavior and Social Processes*, Boston, 1962, pp. 482–505.

19. See, for example, one major effort in this direction which is summarized in Charles E. Ares, Anne Rankin, and Herbert Sturz, "The Manhattan Bail Project: An Interim Report on the Use of Pre-Trial Parole," *New York University Law Review*, January 1963, pp. 67–95.

CHAPTER 4: DISCIPLINE AND PERSPECTIVE IN THE CRIMINAL COURT

1. Amitai Etzioni, *Modern Organizations*, Englewood Cliffs, N. J., 1964, p. 7.

2. James D. Thompson and William J. McEwen, "Organizational Goals and Environment," *American Sociological Review*, XXIII (February 1958), 23–31. The terms "organization" and "bureaucracy" are often used interchangeably, although the former appears to be preferred because of the value-loaded connotations of "bureaucracy" and be-

cause not all organizations are bureaucratic. See Amitai Etzioni, *op. cit.*, p. 3.

3. David Sills, *The Volunteers*, Glencoe, Ill., 1957, p. 64; see also Sheldon L. Messenger, "Organizational Transformation," *American Sociological Review*, XX (February 1955), 3–10, in connection with a similar phenomenon in the Townsend movement.

4. See C. Northcote Parkinson, *Parkinson's Law and Other Studies in Administration*, Boston, 1957, pp. 7–8.

5. Philip Selznick, *TVA and the Grass Roots*, Berkeley, 1949, pp. 196–204.

6. Edward S. Corwin, *op. cit.*, p. 217. See also John Scurlock, "Procedural Protection of the Individual Against the State," *University of Kansas City Law Review*, XXX (Summer 1962), 111–148, for a brief historical statement concerning the origins of the concepts of due process.

7. Morris Janowitz, "Hierarchy and Authority in the Military Establishment," in Amitai Etzioni, ed., *Complex Organizations*, New York, 1961, pp. 211–212.

8. Peter M. Blau and W. Richard Scott, *Formal Organizations*, San Francisco, 1962, pp. 188–189.

9. William M. Evan and Morris Zelditch, Jr., "Experiment on Bureaucratic Authority," *American Sociological Review*, XXVI, No. 6 (December 1961), 892–893.

10. Stanley Milgram, "Behavioral Study of Obedience," *Journal of Abnormal and Social Psychology*, LXVII, No. 4 (1963), 371–378.

11. Robin M. Williams, Jr., *American Society*, 2nd ed. revised, New York, 1960, especially his most notable Chapter X, "Institutional Variation and the Evasion of Normative Patterns," pp. 372–396.

12. George Herbert Mead, "The Psychology of Punitive Justice," *American Journal of Sociology*, XXIII, No. 5 (March 1918), 591.

13. Harold Garfinkel, "Conditions of Successful Degradation Ceremonies," *American Journal of Sociology*, LXI, No. 5 (March 1956), 420–424.

CHAPTER 5: THE LAWYER AS AGENT-MEDIATOR

1. Albert P. Blaustein and Charles O. Porter, *The American Lawyer*, Chicago, 1954, p. 282; Sidney H. Aronson, *Status and Kinship in the Higher Civil Service*, Cambridge, Mass., 1964, p. 39.

2. Andrew Hacker, "Are There Too Many Lawyers in Congress?", *New York Times Magazine*, January 5, 1964, p. 14.

3. Blaustein and Porter, *op. cit.*, p. 97.

4. Joseph A. Schlesinger, "Lawyers and American Politics: A Clarified View," *Midwest Journal of Political Science*, I (May 1957), 26–29.

5. Harlan F. Stone, "The Public Influence of the Bar," *Harvard Law Review,* XLVIII, No. 1 (November 1934), 1–14.
6. William Shakespeare, *King Henry VI,* Part II, Scene II.
7. Carl Sandburg, *The People, Yes,* New York, 1936, p. 164.
8. Thorstein Veblen, *The Theory of the Leisure Class,* New York, 1934, p. 231.
9. Albert J. Reiss, Jr., Otis Dudley Duncan, Paul K. Hatt, and Cecil C. North, *Occupations and Social Status,* New York, 1961; Robert W. Hodge, Paul M. Siegel, and Peter H. Rossi, "Occupational Prestige in the United States, 1925–1963," *American Journal of Sociology,* LXX (November 1964), 286–302.
10. Bernard Barber, *Social Stratification,* New York, 1957, p. 109.
11. Suzanne Keller, *Beyond the Ruling Class,* New York, 1963, p. 325.
12. See Jerome E. Carlin, *Lawyers' Ethics,* New York, 1966, pp. 11–40.
13. Glenn Greenwood, *The 1961 Lawyer Statistical Report,* Chicago, 1961.
14. *1958 Supplement to Lawyers in the United States: Distribution and Income,* Chicago, 1959, pp. 54–55.
15. Jerome E. Carlin, *Lawyers on Their Own,* New Brunswick, N.J., 1962, p. 116.
16. Spencer Klaw, "The Wall Street Lawyers," *Fortune,* February 1958, p. 197.
17. Erwin O. Smigel, "The Impact of Recruitment on the Organization of the Large Law Firm," *American Sociological Review,* XXV, No. 1 (February 1960), 56–66.
18. Harold Laski, *The American Democracy,* New York, 1948, p. 578.
19. Jack Ladinsky, "Careers of Lawyers, Law Practice and Legal Institutions," *American Sociological Review,* XXVIII, No. 1 (February 1963), p. 53; see also Carlin, *Lawyers on Their Own, op. cit.;* Hubert J. O'Gorman, *Lawyers and Matrimonial Cases,* New York, 1963.
20. *New York Times,* October 30, 1964.
21. Erving Goffman, "On Cooling the Mark Out." Goffman's "cooling out" analysis is especially relevant in the lawyer-accused client relationship.

CHAPTER 6: THE JUDGE AS BUREAUCRAT

1. U.S. Bureau of Census, *Statistical Abstract of the United States,* 1964, Washington, D.C., 1964, p. 158.
2. Alex Inkeles and Peter H. Rossi, "National Comparisons of Occupational Prestige," *American Journal of Sociology,* LXI (January 1956), 329–339. See also Robert W. Hodge, Paul M. Siegel, and Peter H. Rossi, *op. cit.,* which indicates that a 1963 replication of the 1947

North-Hatt NORC study of occupational prestige resulted in a correlation of .99, indicating virtually no change in the occupational prestige ratings in the intervening years.

3. *New York Post,* March 8, 1964.
4. Some of the outstanding examples are: Albert J. Beveridge, *The Life of John Marshall,* Boston, 1916; Catherine D. Bowen, *Yankee from Olympus,* Boston, 1944; Samuel J. Konefsky, *Chief Justice Stone and the Supreme Court,* New York, 1945; Alpheus T. Mason, *A Free Man's Life,* New York, 1946, and *Harlan Fiske Stone: Pillar of the Law,* New York, 1956; Carl B. Swisher, *Roger B. Taney,* New York, 1935; Merlo J. Pusey, *Charles Evans Hughes,* New York, 1951; Joel F. Paschal, *Mr. Justice Sutherland: A Man Against the State,* Princeton, 1951; Henry F. Pringle, *The Life and Times of William Howard Taft,* New York, 1939; John P. Frank, *Mr. Justice Black: The Man and His Opinions,* New York, 1949. But see also, by way of contrast, Joseph Borkin, *The Corrupt Judge,* New York, 1962.
5. Wallace S. Sayre and Herbert Kaufman, *Governing New York City,* New York, 1960.
6. John R. Schmidhauser, *The Supreme Court: Its Politics, Personalities, and Procedures,* New York, 1960, pp. 31 and 35.
7. The law school that has no university affiliation is known as a proprietary law school. These were at one time private, profit-making institutions, although most are now chartered as non-profit educational institutions. Even some university affiliated law schools have a "factory"-like character in the number of students in attendance, the curriculum being geared solely to the state's bar examination. See Lowell S. Nicholson, *The Law Schools of the United States,* Baltimore, 1958.
8. Jerome Frank, *Courts on Trial,* Princeton, 1949, Chaps. 11 and 12.
9. Glendon A. Schubert, *Quantitative Analysis of Judicial Behavior,* New York, 1959.
10. See the entire issue entitled "Jurimetrics," *Law and Contemporary Problems* XXVIII, No. 1 (Winter 1963), especially Fred Kort, "Simultaneous Equations and Boulean Algebra in the Analysis of Judicial Decisions," pp. 143–163.
11. Jerome Frank, *Law and the Modern Mind,* Garden City, 1963, p. 112. See also Joseph C. Hutcheson, "The Judgment Intuitive: The Function of the 'Hunch' in Judicial Decisions," *Cornell Law Quarterly,* XIV (1929), 274–278.
12. Oliver Wendell Holmes, *The Common Law,* Boston, 1881, p. 35.
13. Abraham S. Blumberg and Charles Winick, "The Appellate Judge," unpublished study.

CHAPTER 7: PROBATION AND PSYCHIATRY

1. David Dressler, *Practice and Theory of Probation and Parole,* New York, 1959, p. 7.
2. Mary Richmond, *Social Diagnosis,* New York, 1917, p. 51.
3. Herbert H. Apteker, *The Dynamics of Casework and Counseling,* Boston, 1955, pp. 41–70.
4. Edmond Fitzgerald, "The Presentence Investigation," in Barbara A. Kay and Clyde B. Vedder, eds., *Probation and Parole,* Springfield, Ill., 1963, p. 35.
5. Manfred Guttmacher, "Status of Adult Court Psychiatric Clinics," *National Probation and Parole Association Journal,* I (October 1955), 97–105.
6. *Williams vs. New York,* 337 U.S. 241 (1949).
7. Thomas S. Szasz, *Law, Liberty and Psychiatry,* New York, 1963, p. 32.
8. For a keen analysis of some of the medico-legal problems involved in connection with psychiatry in the court setting, see Thomas S. Szasz, *Psychiatric Justice,* New York, 1965; also Thomas J. Scheff, "The Societal Reaction to Deviance," *Social Problems,* II (Spring 1964), 401–413, with reference to commitment proceedings, wherein psychiatrists tend to exercise a rather strong presumption in favor of the existence of mental illness in the course of their professional service in that setting; Joyce D. Chaikin, "Commitment by Fiat: New York's New Mental Hygiene Law," *Columbia Journal of Law and Social Problems,* I, No. 1 (June 1965), 113–124.
9. John Dickinson, *Administrative Justice and the Supremacy of Law in the United States,* New York, 1959, pp. 39–75.
10. Paul W. Tappan, *Crime, Justice and Correction,* New York, 1960, p. 465.
11. Charles L. Chute and Marjorie Bell, *Crime, Courts and Probation,* New York, 1956, p. 190.
12. The amount of the workload fluctuates from court to court within a given state, and even within a court over a period of time. But sixteen to twenty "investigations" per month are a quite common work load. In many courts a probation worker is also carrying an "under care" case load, in addition to his investigation responsibilities.
13. Robert K. Merton, *Mass Persuasion,* New York, 1946, p. 142.
14. *Williams vs. New York,* 337 U.S. 241 (1949), at p. 249.

CHAPTER 8: THE CONVERGENCE OF THE ADVERSARY AND BUREAUCRATIC MODELS

1. Paul Tappan, *Juvenile Delinquency,* New York, 1949, pp. 204–205; see also Margaret Rosenheim, *Justice for the Child,* New York, 1962.
2. On May 15, 1967, in a landmark decision by the United States Supreme Court *In the Matter of Gault,* most of the procedural due process requirements of the adult criminal courts (notice of charges, right to counsel, right to confront accusers and witnesses, adequate notice of the privilege against self-incrimination) were made applicable to the juvenile courts. See also COMMENT, "Criminal Offenders in the Juvenile Court: More Brickbats and Another Proposal," *University of Pennsylvania Law Review,* CXIV (June 1966), 1171–1220.
3. Etzioni, *Modern Organizations,* p. 19.
4. Richard J. Whalen, "A City Destroying Itself," *Fortune,* September 1964, p. 116.
5. Andrew Hacker, "Power to Do What?", in Irving L. Horowitz, ed., *The New Sociology,* New York, 1964.
6. *New York Times,* November 8, 1966.
7. See Dominick R. Vetri, NOTE, "Guilty Plea Bargaining: Compromises by Prosecutors to Secure Guilty Pleas," *University of Pennsylvania Law Review,* CXII (April 1964), 865–895.

Index

Accused, 4–7, 9–11, 21–31 *passim*, 33–35, 40, 46–47, 78, 81, 96, 103–105, 108, 111–114, 141, 146–149, 157–159, 161–162, 167, 170, 172–175, 177, 179, 181, 183; career in criminal court, 53–59, 61–71, 86–94, 113; fear of jury trials, 55–59; number of, 9–10; protection and rights of, 8, 14–17, 21–26, 65, 95–96 (*see also* Due process; Rights and safeguards for individuals); sifting of, 51–56. *See also* Defendant; Youth; Youthful Offender.

Acquittals, 28, 31–32, 54, 112, 174, 175

Adjudications, 53–54, 171–172, 176

Adler, Alfred, 144

Agent-mediator roles, 65–69, 78, 91–94, 95–115, 173, 179

American Bar Association, 11, 102, 122

American Bar Foundation, 10, 28, 100

American Dilemma, An (Myrdal), 3

Appeals, 9

Arraignment, 22; pre-arraignment stage, 23; preliminary arraignment, 54

Arrests, 5, 9–10, 22–24, 27, 51, 53–54, 183; promise of immunity, 24

Attorneys. *See* Lawyers; District attorney.

Bail system, 10, 33, 37, 58, 59, 68–69, 111, 175–177

Bar, 97, 103, 118, 123; bar examination, 119, 124

Bentham, Jeremy, 86. *See also* Panopticon effect.

Bill of Rights, applicability to federal and state defendants, 13–16. *See also* Constitutional amendments; Due process; Rights and safeguards; Supreme Court decisions.

Black, Justice Hugo, 15

Blau, Peter, 79–80

Bleuler, Eugen, 148

Bronx County Bar Association, 6

Bryce, James, 101

Budgets, 49, 50; of district attorney's office, 44; of legal-aid defender office, 43–44; of Metropolitan Court, 41–43; of probation division, 146

Canons of Judicial Ethics: Canon 14, 128; Canon 28, 122, 128
Cases, criminal, 15, 21, 24, 58, 67, 96, 148; disposition of, 6, 9, 21, 27–32, 55, 59, 67, 68, 96, 103–104, 144–145, 160, 172–175, 179; workload of, 6, 21, 45, 50, 53, 60, 65, 103–104, 127, 157, 159, 179. *See also* Criminal process.
Cases, federal, 13
Cicourel, Aaron, 49
Civil service, 41–42, 44–45, 81, 108, 124; civil service malaise, 154–162
Clerk's office, of criminal court, 41–42, 47, 87, 108, 124
Coercion, 5–7, 17–21 *passim,* 23–24, 85, 89. *See also* Manipulation.
Complainant, 64, 87, 105, 145, 160, 166
Complicity by authority, organized system of, 78, 83–86
Confessions, 6–7, 23–24, 92, 93, 96, 182, 183. *See also* Pleas, negotiated.
Congress, 18; lawyers in, 97, 99
Constitution, 3, 25, 145
Constitutional amendments, 13–17, 24, 171; Fourth Amendment, 14, 24; Fifth Amendment, 14, 24, 96; Sixth Amendment, 14, 25; Eighth Amendment, 14; Fourteenth Amendment, 13–15. *See also* Due process; Justice; Rights and safeguards; Rule of law; Supreme Court decisions.
Constitutional issues, Executive Order 9066, 18, 21
Constitutional renovation, federal-state procedural gaps, 22. *See also* Supreme Court decisions.

Convictions, 28, 31–32, 36, 46, 51, 53–55, 57, 58, 64–65, 114, 129, 145, 161, 171, 173–175, 177; of judges for bribery, 118. *See also* Adjudications.
"Cop-out" ceremony, 21, 88–89, 91, 105, 131; transcript of, 131–136. *See also* Pleas, negotiated.
Counsel. *See* Lawyers.
Court of Appeals, 9
Court of Star Chamber, 23
Courts, 7–8, 13, 27, 35, 44, 58, 102, 117–123; English, 147. *See also* Criminal court; Juvenile court; Metropolitan Court.
Crater, Judge, 117
Crime, 11, 22–25 *passim,* 27–28, 30, 35, 36, 46, 50–51, 53, 89, 111, 143, 147, 158, 166, 169, 170, 172–173; statistics, 9–10
"Criminal," 9, 34, 35, 39, 64, 88, 127, 170–172, 175; "non-criminal," 170–172. *See also* Youthful Offender.
Criminal appeals, 25
Criminal conduct, 8, 51
Criminal court, 7–11, 13, 22, 31, 47, 61, 64, 96, 103, 109, 118, 119–120, 122–125, 130, 146, 169, 172; administration of, 11, 59, 140, 181 (*see also* Judges, board of); adult, 4, 145, 170–172, 174–175; ameliorative-therapeutic techniques, 34–36, 62, 171–172, 175, 181 (*see also* Criminal court process, young adults); bureaucratic authority in, 5, 46, 50, 59, 62, 78–88, 129, 130, 171, 177, 180–181; clients of, 11, 32, 34, 49, 50, 81–82; as "closed community" (social structure), 49, 59, 61, 70, 86–87, 139, 182; ideology of, 5, 21, 32–37, 73–74 (*see also* Due process); legal system of, 21, 34, 61–63 *passim;* four levels of, 8–10; occupational personnel of, 4, 5, 32, 34–37, 42–43, 50, 62, 85–86, 94, 104, 108, 112, 114, 130, 147, 155–156, 179, 183 (*see also*

Clerk's office; District attorney's office; Judges; Legal-aid defender service; Probation division; Psychiatric clinic); procedures, 6, 59, 171 (*see also* Due process; Constitutional amendments; Rights and safeguards; Supreme Court decisions); as social problem, 3–12. *See also* Justice, criminal; Metropolitan Court.

Criminal court communication and organization structure, 4–6, 11, 32, 33–34, 37, 39–71 *passim,* 74–75, 96, 104–106, 112–114, 124, 137–143, 153, 155–161, 177–179, 180–184; aims of, 5–6, 37, 61, 74–78, 124, 138, 170, 172, 178–179; discipline and perspective of, 71, 73–94, 114, 140, 179

Criminal court process, 9, 21–22, 25, 51, 59, 110, 175; of young adults, 172–177. *See also* Criminal process.

Criminal court system, 6, 32, 47, 59, 63. *See also* Agent-mediator roles; Justice, criminal.

Criminal law, 4, 11, 76, 109, 124, 127; administration of, 17, 21–22, 35–36, 55, 76, 92, 95, 140; constitutional elements of, 5, 16 (*see also* Due process); in Russia, 19, 37. *See also* Law.

Criminal procedure, 6–8, 35; administration of, 14; constitutional requirements of, 14–17; federal, 13–17. *See also* Due process; Supreme Court decisions.

Criminal process, 21–25, 28–29, 40, 43, 49; sieve effect in, 27, 40, 50–55, 63–71

Criminal record: juvenile, 171–172; prior, 57, 91, 105, 145, 160; Youthful Offender, 173

Criminal responsibility, 76. *See also* Insanity, legal.

Criminal statistics, 9–11, 51–52

Criminal violations. *See* Felony; Misdemeanor.

Criminals, "white-collar," 40–41, 57

Criminology, 34–37, 41; Positivist school of, 34–35

Cross-examination, 146, 162

Darrow, Clarence, 101

Declaration of Independence, 97

Defendant, 5–7, 9–11, 24, 27–28, 30, 31, 33, 37, 40, 55, 57–59, 65, 67–70, 81–82, 85, 89–94, 104, 111, 114, 129, 136, 142, 145–148, 157–160, 166, 170, 172, 175, 179, 182–183; federally accused, 15; indigent, 24–25, 95, 103–105 *passim,* 183; legal rights of, 6, 14–17, 21–25, 95–96; role of, 57, 89–94. *See also* Rights and safeguards.

Defense, 26, 31, 56, 175

Delinquents, 11, 36, 51, 171

Deviants, 19, 35, 39–40, 61–62

Deterrence and punishment, 76

Diagnostic testing, 43, 143–145, 149; reports of, 149–152, 162–163; transcripts of, 163–166. *See also* Probation division; Psychiatry.

District attorney, 28, 44–46, 51, 58–61, 64–68, 81–82, 86–87, 90, 92, 94, 96, 104, 106, 114, 129, 131, 137, 141, 145, 170, 175, 179, 183; agent-mediator role, 66, 68; assistant, 44–46, 64, 66, 105, 125; office of, 44–47, 66, 86–87, 105, 108–109, 125, 139, 141; personnel, 44–45; pressures on, 59–61; procedures of, 59. *See also* Prosecution.

Due process of law, 7, 25, 32, 61, 62, 75, 77, 78, 129, 153, 166, 169, 170–172, 178, 180, 181, 184; "bureaucratic due process," 4, 5, 21, 26, 29, 37, 169–170, 172, 177; constitutional and Supreme Court requirements, 4–6, 8, 14–17, 20–23, 26, 70, 145–146, 172, 177, 183; dissonance of principles and practice, 26–34, 37, 70; ideology of, 32–33, 170; instrument of coercion, 17–21, 89; statutory vagueness, 22; violations of, 22, 24, 35–37, 89, 146, 171. *See also* Constitutional amendments; Rights and safeguards; Supreme Court decisions.

Escobedo vs. Illinois (1964), 23, 95–96
Etzioni, Amitai, 74, 177–178
Evan, William, 82
Execution, 8, 55, 137, 146
Executive Order 9066, 18

Federal Bureau of Investigation, 9–10, 51
Federal criminal proceedings, regulation of, 14–17. *See also* Constitutional amendments; Supreme Court decisions.
Felony, 8–9, 11, 27–29, 40, 43, 51–54 *passim,* 56–57, 95, 105, 112, 173, 183
Frankfurter, Justice Felix, 15
Freud, Sigmund, 144, 148

Garfinkel, Harold, 88
German juridical and bureaucratic apparatus, under Nazis, 19–20
Gideon vs. Wainwright (1963), 43, 95–96, 103
Goffman, Erving, 63–64, 68
Goldstein, Abraham S., 148
Grand jury, 25, 27, 29, 51, 53–54. *See also* Indictment.
Guilt, 4, 5, 13, 18, 20, 23–24, 30, 88–92, 166, 173, 181, 184; determination of, 23, 26, 36, 46, 143, 170–173; presumption of, 6, 7, 27, 69; prove beyond a reasonable doubt, 25, 27, 105, 171. *See also* Pleadings.

Hacker, Andrew, 180
Hand, Justice Learned, 117
Hearings, 22, 51; judicial, 5; preliminary, 9
Hilberg, Raul, 19

Holmes, Justice Oliver Wendell, 123, 128

Immunity, 65, 147
Indictment, 27, 29, 31, 53–58, 104, 172, 175, 182; multiple-count, 56–58, 64; transcript of, 56–57
Individualization, 4, 26, 34, 76, 146, 160, 170, 172, 177; myth of, 170, 172
Informers, 64; mistrust of, 25
Innocence, 4, 5, 18, 20, 21, 26, 30, 36, 89–92; determination of, 26, 36, 170–171, 173, 179, 181; presumption of, 4, 6, 25, 27, 37, 51, 62, 172–173. *See also* Pleadings.
Inquisition, reaction to, 23
Insanity, legal concept of, 36, 147–148
Interrogation, 23

Janowitz, Morris, 78
Japanese-Americans, exclusion and removal, 17–18
Judge, 27, 34, 36, 44, 60–61, 64–66 *passim,* 68, 77, 81–82, 86–88, 94, 96, 106, 108, 113–114, 145–146, 149, 157, 170, 173, 179, 181, 183; agent-mediator role, 65; in bargain plea process, 58–61, 65–66, 68, 104–105; as bureaucrat, 117–142; number and distribution of, 117; status of, 117–118. *See also* Judicial career; Judicial decision-making; Metropolitan Court, judges of.
Judges, Board of, 41, 86, 87
Judicial career, 118–123, 127, 137, 140–141; income, 41, 123; lower level, 119–121; middle level, 121; upper level, 122–123; retirement, 124; socio-demographic variables, 124–126
Judicial decision-making, 41, 58, 124, 126–137, 145–149, 152–153, 157–158, 160, 162; ambivalence toward rules, 127–129; budget-

making, 130; effect of background, 127–128; influence of probation and psychiatric reports, 145–149, 152–153, 157–158, 160, 162; overseer of guilty pleas, 130–136; practice of sentencing, 136–137

Judicial role performance, patterns of, 137–142

Judicial trial, 5, 173

Juridical systems, 19–20

Jurisprudence, system of, 17, 25, 29, 45, 77, 128, 183

Jury: decline of system, 4, 55–56, 58; hung, 31–32, 170; manipulation by judge, 142; trial by, 4, 29, 30–32, 55–59, 61, 69, 129, 142, 145–146, 147, 182; waived, 70. *See also* Trial.

"Justice," 3, 15–17, 19, 22, 33, 46, 74–75, 77–78, 129, 160, 178, 181

Justice, administration of, 6, 27, 137, 141, 178

Justice, criminal, 4, 7, 8, 11, 14, 25–27, 70, 119, 167, 169, 170, 178–179, 182, 184; accusatorial system of, 6, 22, 103; adversary system of, 4–6, 13–37, 66, 96, 114, 148, 167, 169, 170, 177, 181, 184 (*see also* Due process); adversary system converging with bureaucratic system, 169–184; assembly-line system of, 5–7, 24, 170; bargaining system of, 64–65, 177, 179, 182; inquisitorial system of, 103; by negotiation, 21, 30, 33, 53–65, 70, 177–179; system without trial, 27, 33, 182

Juvenile courts, 9–10, 11, 36, 170–173. *See also* Criminal court process, young adults.

Kamisar, Yale, 7

Kaufman, Herbert, 120

Keller, Suzanne, 99

Kent, Chancellor James, 128

Keogh, Judge J. Vincent, convicted of bribery, 118

Kings County Criminal Court, Brooklyn, 53–54

Korematsu Case, 18

Laski, Harold, 101

Law, 13, 19, 34–37, 58, 65, 77, 140, 153, 154; administration of, 118, 124; careers and services, 98–109; enforcement, 19, 22, 26, 50–51, 56, 96, 156, 162, 183; practice of, 46, 47, 85, 99, 100, 102, 104, 106–107, 119–123, 125–127; practice as confidence game, 110–115; schools, 44, 99, 107, 109, 119, 121–122, 124, 125, 127, 139

Lawyers, 6, 28, 34, 37, 42–43, 47, 50, 59, 60–61, 65, 77, 81, 85–87, 97, 103–109, 117, 112–113, 123, 127, 128, 139, 158; constitutional, 25; criminal court "regulars," 60–61, 66, 104–108, 123; in government service, 97, 99, 104; income of, 100–101, 106, 109; judicial/political aspirants, 118–122, 128; in Metropolitan Court, 103–109; number and distribution of, 100, 103; specialization of, 101–102; ties with big business, 101–103

Lawyers, defense, 23, 27–28, 33, 47, 55, 60–61, 64–66, 68, 85–86, 89, 92–94, 110, 119, 131, 139, 141, 142, 146, 148, 170, 173, 176, 179, 181, 183; agent-mediator role, 66, 68, 92–94, 95–115, 173, 179; fixing and collecting fees, 66, 85, 97, 110–114; pressures on, 64–65; relations with clients, 47, 66, 85–86, 92–94, 110, 112–113; reputation of, 96–98; self-image, 106

Legal-aid, 24–25, 93–94; types of, 103

Legal-aid defender service, 28, 43–44, 46, 108; in Metropolitan Court, 103–105, 108

Legal institutions, 76

Legal proceeding. *See* Due process.

Legal system, 19–20, 96, 118

Legislature, 99

Leyra vs. Denno (1954), 24
Litigation, 102, 113, 127

Magistrates, 22, 120
Magna Carta, 77
Manipulation, discipline and authority through, 10, 23, 78–82, 90, 91, 93, 111, 113, 119, 140, 142, 158, 161, 179, 183
Manton, federal judge, convicted of bribery, 117–118
Marshall, Justice John, 123
McNabb-Mallory rule, 22
McNaghten rule: "right-wrong" test, 147. *See also* Insanity, legal.
Mead, George Herbert, 88
Merton, Robert K., 161
Metropolitan Court, 10, 28–30, 32, 37, 40–43, 44, 53–55, 56, 59, 60, 66, 76, 89–90, 93–94; budget, 41–43; case load and distribution, 53–55, 103–104, 137–139; judges of, 41, 50, 120, 123, 124–131, 137–142; lawyers of, 103–109, 120, 158; organization and goals, 41–43, 76; personnel, 41–43, 50; political nature of structure, 41–42; probation division, 40–43, 47, 59, 87, 89, 129, 154–161; psychiatric clinic, 43, 149, 152, 154, 162; size of, 10, 40; youth section, 174–177
Milgram, Stanley, 82–83
Mills, C. Wright, 180
Miranda vs. Arizona (1966), 23, 96
Misdemeanors, 8, 10, 11, 28, 54, 57, 58, 173
Myrdal, Gunnar, 3

National Opinion Research Center, 98
New York Criminal Court, 6
New York Times, 6
News media, 47, 61, 69, 118, 140–141
Nosological categories, 36, 148

Obedience, discipline and authority through, 78, 82–83
Osterman, Judge Melvin L., convicted of bribery, 118

Packer, Herbert L., 6
Panopticon effect, discipline and authority through, 78, 86–88
Parole, 176–177; officers, 91
Pleading, pleas, 41, 46, 66–68, 88–89, 91–92, 105, 112–113, 119, 131, 139, 149, 157, 177, 179, 183; bargain plea process, 55, 104–105, 136, 183; guilty plea, 5, 6, 37, 64, 89, 90–92, 114, 130, 136, 148, 182; guilty, lesser offense, 58, 64, 88, 89, 105, 113, 131, 139, 161, 179, 183; guilty plea practice, 28–31, 45, 50, 53; pressure for guilty pleas, 4–6, 28–31, 37, 51, 55–63, 68, 88–94, 113, 183; negotiated plea, 21, 30, 55, 58, 59, 64–68, 108, 112, 128, 131, 183; "not guilty," 68; plea before trial, 5, 28–29, 31, 54, 129, 130–131; prepleading investigation, 104, 147, 177. *See also* "Cop-out" ceremony; Justice, by negotiation.
Police, 7, 10, 17, 22, 26, 27, 50–51, 53, 56, 59–61, 64–68, 87, 90, 92–96 *passim,* 108, 131, 145, 146, 166, 170, 179, 181, 183; agent-mediator role, 65, 68; investigation, 24, 51, 95–96; manuals, 23; pressures on, 59
Political influence and pressure, 21, 59, 67, 127, 137, 139, 140, 160, 170, 182; clubhouse ties, 44, 45, 105, 119–121, 125, 128, 130, 140–141; political patronage system, 41–42, 44, 45, 46, 119–122, 125–126, 155
Political myths, 32–33, 126
Prisons, 8, 11, 35–36, 57, 59, 60, 68, 69, 86, 112, 113. 136, 145, 176, 179, 183; remand prison, 68; warden, 60, 179
Probable cause, 24, 27

Probation, 58, 76, 91, 129, 143–153, 159, 175; career in, 154–161; effect on courts and judges, 143–153; function of, 144; personnel, 34–37, 61–63 *passim,* 65–68, 80–81, 85, 87, 89, 91, 104, 108, 139, 141, 144, 146, 147, 154, 181, 183; professional status, 156–158. *See also* Civil service malaise.

Probation and psychiatry, 143–167

Probation reports, 67, 129, 137, 143–147, 149, 157–158, 160–163, 166, 170, 172, 173, 175; reliance upon, 67, 90, 129, 137, 143–147, 160; transcripts of, 163–166

Prosecution, 7, 10, 25, 26, 27, 31, 40, 44, 45, 50, 58, 96, 103–105, 177, 181, 182. *See also* District attorney.

Psychiatric reports, 36, 67, 137, 147–149, 166, 170, 172, 173, 175; reliance on, 67, 137

Psychiatry, 24, 33–37, 43, 63, 65, 67–68, 76, 79–81, 86, 143–153, 154, 159, 161, 181; agent-mediator role, 67–68; effect on court organization and judge's decisions, 143–153; occupational voyeurism, 159; testimony at trial, 147–148

"Psychoauthoritarianism," 35

Psychological personnel, 62–63, 154

Psychological reports, reliance upon, 173, 175, 181

Punishment, 8, 18, 20, 35, 36, 55, 59, 65, 76, 87, 105, 137, 169, 170, 179

Rank, Otto, 144

Rehabilitation and reformation, 76, 181

Rights and safeguards for individuals, 3, 5, 6, 8, 14–17, 22–25, 27, 65, 147, 171, 173, 177; privilege against self-incrimination, 14, 17, 23–24, 36, 96, 173; prohibition against cruel and unusual punishment, 14, 25; prohibition against double jeopardy, 14; prohibition against unreasonable search and seizure, 14, 24; right to assistance of counsel, 14, 22, 24–25, 27, 95–96, 171 (*see also* Defendant, indigent); right to confront and cross-examine accusers, witnesses, 14, 25, 171; right to impartial judge, 25; right to impartial prosecutor, 25, 45; right to indictment by grand jury, 14, 22, 29, 30, 171; right to reasonable bail, 14, 25; right to remain silent, 22, 24, 96; right to trial by jury, 14, 25, 29, 36; rights waived by Youthful Offender, 177. *See also* Due process; Constitutional amendments; Supreme Court decisions.

Rome, legal system of, 19

Rule of law, 4, 5, 16, 20, 74, 77, 78, 169; instrument of coercion, 17–21

Russia, legal system of, 19, 37

Sandburg, Carl, 98; *The People, Yes,* 95

Sayre, Wallace, 120

Scott, Richard, 79–80

Self-incrimination, 14, 17, 23–24, 36, 96, 173, 175

Selznick, Philip, 76

Sentence, 5, 28, 31, 36, 41, 57–59 *passim,* 65, 68, 87, 89, 91, 105, 108, 112, 113, 128, 129, 136–137, 139, 145–146, 149, 157, 160, 172, 177; pre-sentence probation investigation and reports, 143–147, 153, 157–158, 160–166; sentencing procedure, 128; suspended sentence, 58

Skolnick, Jerome, 27

Sobel, Justice Nathan R., 53

Social scientists, 179

Sociologists, 40, 49, 50, 63, 153

Social work, 61, 67, 76, 79–80, 144, 154–156, 170, 173, 181; pre-hearing investigation of Youthful Offender, 173

Statutory provisions, 128

Stone, Chief Justice Harlan F., 98
Supreme court, state, 9
Supreme Court of the United States, 9, 18, 20, 25, 103, 181–182; decisions of, 23, 95–96, 145–146, 153, 157, 166, 183, 184; historical position on Bill of Rights and criminal law, 13–17, 21, 22 (*see also* Constitutional amendments; Due process); justices of, 13, 18, 99, 122
Suspects, 23, 38, 95–96
Szasz, Thomas, 148, 173

Tappan, Paul, 153, 171
Tennessee Valley Authority, 76
Tocqueville, Alexis de, 97, 101
Trials, 9, 24, 25, 27–31, 36, 50, 55, 58–59, 61, 64–65, 69, 89, 92, 104, 112, 129, 139, 147, 148, 172–173; pressure to avoid, 27–30, 58, 129;

pre-trial examination and investigation, 37, 172, 174; for Youthful Offender, 172–173

Uniform Crime Reports, 10

Veblen, Thorstein, 98

Warren, Chief Justice Earl, 103
Weber, Max, 46, 73, 78; "rational-legal" authority, 78–88, 93. *See also* Complicity; Manipulation; Obedience; Panopticon effect.
Wiretapping, 6
Witnesses, 33, 56

Youth, in court, 170–171
Youthful Offender, 54, 172–177. *See also* Criminal court process, young adult.

Zelditch, Morris, 82

A note on the author

Abraham S. Blumberg was born in New York City and studied at Brooklyn College and the Columbia University School of Law. He was admitted to the New York Bar in 1947 and to the Bar of the United States Supreme Court in 1961, while engaged in general practice with an emphasis upon criminal and constitutional law. He also served as counsel for the Institute of Human Relations. When he turned to sociology, he studied and received a Ph.D. at the New School for Social Research. He has since served as research consultant to the President's Committee on Juvenile Delinquency and is now Associate Professor of Sociology and Law at John Jay College of the City University of New York. Mr. Blumberg lives in Bayside, New York, with his wife and two children.

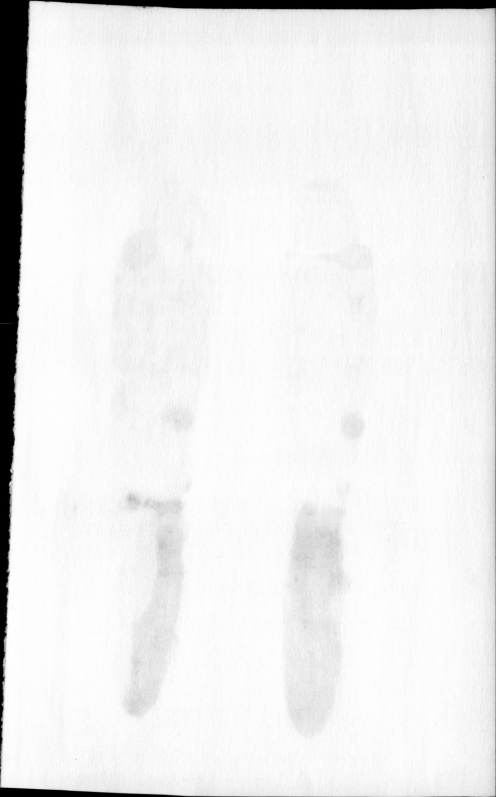